With Hitler for
Mother Russia

Perry Pierik

With Hitler for Mother Russia

The History of
Soviet patriotic Collaborators

Aspekt Publishing

With Hitler for Mother Russia

© Perry Pierik
© 2023 Publisher ASPEKT
Amersfoortsestraat 27, 3769 AD Soesterberg, Netherlands
info@uitgeverijaspekt.nl - www.uitgeverijaspekt.nl

Cover design: Aspekt Graphics
Inside: Sjoerd van 't Slot
Translated by: Isabel Oomen

ISBN: 9789464628692
NUR: 680

All rights reserved. No part of this publication may be reproduced, stored in a retrieval system or transmitted in any form or by any means, electronic, mechanical, photocopying, recording or otherwise, without the prior permission of the publisher.

As far as the making of copies from this publication is permitted on the basis of Article 16B Auteurswet 1912 (Dutch Copyright Act of 1912), the Decree of 20 June 1974, no. 351, as amended by the Decree of 23 August 1985, no. 471, and Article 17 Auteurswet 1912 (Dutch Copyright Act of 1912), the legally owed fees for this must be paid to Stichting Reprorecht (Box 882, 1180 AW, Amstelveen, The Netherlands). For the reproduction of part(s) of this publication in anthologies, readers and other compilation works (article 16 Auteurswet 1912), the publisher should be contacted.

Table of contents

Introduction	7
Kress von Kressenstein in Georgia	9
Consequences of the Russian Revolution	13
Approximation of Moscow and Berlin via Rapello	20
Ukraine and Pavlo Skoropadsky	23
Holodomor, Starvation of the Ukraine	25
Murder on the Coolsingel	29
Stepan Bandera, "Ehrenhaft" and Operation "Barbarossa	32
Establishment of Units and Militias as of June 1941	39
Osttruppen in Trawniki and elsewhere	45
'I see this as decisive for the war'	48
Theodor Oberländer	52
Amin el Husseini	54
Murderous Ukrainian Militias	57
The Discovery of Andrei Vlassov	62
Opportunities in the Kalmüken steppe	66
Oberländer Notes Murders in Taman	70

Stalingrad Offers Vlassov chances	72
Tiresome Road After the Fields of Prokhorovka	78
Himmler Discovers the Possibilities of Collaboration	82
The SS becomes Vlassov's "ally" and the Establishment of "Neu Turkestan	85
The Division "Galizien", between war crimes and soldier's courage	92
Increasing desertion	97
Vlassov's Late Triumph in Hradschin Palace	100
The Seed of Truth and its Fruit	103
The "breeding ground" of Soviet Citizens in German Hand	107
Himmler tests 'his' Russians on the Oder	110
Melancholy in the Battle of Erlenhof	112
Vlassov Collects his Troops near Prague	116
Loyalty to Germany or Hand in Hand with The Czech Resistance?	119
Battles around Rosin between Vlassov Army and the Germans	123
The GIs in Pilsen	127
Swallowed up by Yalta	129
Afterword: Difficult Balance Sheet	133
Concise literature Review:	135

Introduction

Approximately one million inhabitants of the Soviet Union collaborated with the Nazis. This is a remarkable fact because the Nazis can not exactly be seen as allies due to their racial policy. And yet it happened. Through aversion to Bolshevism, hope for new freedom, patriotism and a slowly forming understanding among forces on the German side, a new horizon emerged in which collaboration between the Soviet peoples and the Germans might offer a better alternative to the 'Soviet paradise'. Historical oppression and experiences played a major role in this, especially in Ukraine, amidst the Crimea and the Caucasus peoples, but also among the Russians who longed for the tsarist times of old.

This led to a difficult but ultimately large-scale collaboration. Using documents and literature, an insight is given into the broad outlines of this extraordinary event. It is a dramatic fact, since the collapse of the Third Reich meant the Osttruppen's pursuit of freedom was called into question and met a dark end.

The history of the 'Osttruppen' has therefore been surrounded by discussion and emotion to this day and belongs in the deepest, darkest caves of the war. This book focuses on the collaboration of the Soviet peoples on the Eastern Front. It is a limited preliminary study of a larger book on which the author is currently working.

This is a first *Outline History* where a wider audience can become acquainted with this phenomenon. In connection with this, it is good to refer to other literature by the author of this book, such as *Neu Turkestan aan het front*, in which Islamic collaboration is discussed.

Kress von Kressenstein in Georgia

He was a remarkable figure, the German General Friedrich Kress von Kressenstein, when he crossed the Georgian border in 1918 at the head of a German military unit. His sharply cut face had militaristic features, but his sophisticated glasses also betrayed a sharp intellect. The First World War had ended for Russia with the Treaty of Brest-Litovsk. As a result of the Great October Revolution, chaos reigned in the gigantic Russian empire. The balance of power shifted and peoples saw an opportunity to develop their national identity. This also offered new opportunities for Germany and for Berlin's relationship with the East.

Friedrich Kress von Kressenstein, born in Nuremberg in April 1870 - the year of the Franco-Prussian War - had an extraordinary career behind him. Fate had connected him with the (Middle) East. The artillery general had been active in the Ottoman Empire before the First World War. He was part of the Liman von Sanders mission to Turkey. This cooperation was of great importance for Wilhelminian Germany. Turkey was strategically situated between the Middle East and Central Asia and also guarded strategic waterways. By July 1914, an understanding had formed between Constantinople and Berlin with regard to Tsarist Russia. The Turks sought military backing from the Germans and

Kress von Kressenstein

the Austro-Hungarian double monarchy. In particular, technical support regarding the high-grade German military-industrial complex. Kress von Kressenstein had played a not insignificant role in this matter and had been honoured by the Turkish authorities with the high distinction of 'Imtiyaz Madalyasi', the so-called 'Order of Honour' with the 'golden swords'. Von Kressenstein wore this high award with pride on a triangular ribbon, unlike the Prussian officers who wore such medals pinned to their chests. In this way he emphasized his Bavarian descent.

In Russia, revolution had come in October 1917. The proud Tsarist Empire had been greatly weakened by the moral bankruptcy of the regime and the disappointing results at the front, leaving it vulnerable to the revolutionary elements in the country. From recent studies, among others by the German historian Eva Ingeborg Fleischhauer, we know that there had long been connections between Lenin and other revolutionaries in and outside the Tsarist Empire, who now saw their chance. In collaboration with certain sections of the German military high command, the OHL, and officers around the influential General Erich Ludendorff, the revolution was meticulously prepared. When Lenin moved in the sealed train from Germany via Scandinavia to St. Petersburg, people at the OHL spoke of 'our man in Russia'. This was a role that the vain Lenin did not like at all. As a communist revolutionary, he did not want to be a puppet of the 'capitalist powers' and communist historiography left the German role with regard to the revolution from the history books.

Erich Ludendorff

After the collapse of the Empire in November 1918, Germany purged its own archives. They did not want to be held responsible for the bloody social experiment that had been set in motion by the Russian Revolution. All this did not alter the fact that the German involvement in the geopolitical developments in the East was considerable.

Consequences of the Russian Revolution

In the short term, the Russian Revolution seemed to bring benefits to the German Empire. The revolution had brought forces to power that did not see any point in continuing the First World War. On 3 March 1918, the war on the Eastern Front was officially ended by the Peace of Brest-Litovsk, where peace was signed between the so-called Central Powers (Germany, Austria-Hungary, Bulgaria and the Ottoman Empire) and the representatives of Bolshevik Russia.

For Vladimir Lenin, Leon Trotsky and the other Bolshevik leaders, Brest-Litovsk was simply a way of getting a free hand. It was clear that the Russian Revolution was more of a coup than a revolution and that soon, they would have their hands full fighting the restorative forces that were trying to put the House of Romanov and the old regime back in the saddle.

As a result of the collapse of the tsarist empire, all kinds of nationalist elements within the 'vielvölker' empire of Russia also regained momentum. The idea of liberation reigned supreme. This was supported by the message of American President Thomas Woodrow Wilson, who spoke of the right of self-determination. In the West, attention was focused on the Austro-Hungarian Empire. The dual monarchy was the 'vielvölker' state par excellence, and now the Empire was falling apart. The old Emperor, Franz Joseph, died in the war and his second cousin, Karl I, had only just ascended the throne and lacked authority. Even former wing Adjutant Miklos Horthy turned his back on Vienna and an independent Hungary, after first withstanding a communist coup attempt led by the journalist and Lenin confidant Béla Kun. Other nations, too, rose from the ashes to take advantage of the situation, such as the Polish, Czechs, Slovaks, Croats and Slovenes. The same process took place in the east of Russia. Georgia was one of the first to restore its own religious authority in the country in March 1917, heralding further political and cultural unrest. Further disintegration was followed by new steps and mass desertion from the tsarist army. Two forces came to oppose each other: the Bolsheviks versus the Nationalists.

In the Caucasian region, there was initially a miraculous interim solution, the so-called Transcaucasian Commissariat, to which, apart from Georgia, Armenia and Azerbaijan also belonged. However, this artificial link did not last long and shortly afterwards, in May 1918, Georgia declared independence. This major step was reason for both the government in Tbilisi and in Berlin to shuffle the strategic cards again. Georgia, of course, feared interference from the communists and was eagerly looking for allies. This was the reason why Kress von Kressenstein's 3000-strong force entered Georgia; in the hope that this German backing would give strength to the pursuit of sovereignty. For Berlin, the country was close to the strategic Caucasian oil fields and the Black Sea coastline and therefore of great importance.

Georgia's move to independence had a snowball effect on other states. Armenia and Azerbaijan followed a few days later. Despite the triumphant and symbolic entry of the German troops, the Caucasian adventure of Wilhelmina Germany was short-lived. The Treaty of Brest-Litovsk had been used to move troops from the Eastern Front to the Western Front, but the German spring offensive of 1918 it made possible, was not as successful as hoped. Led by Paul of Hindenburg and Erich Ludendorff, the German divisions had moved in on 21 March. Under the code name 'Michael', the offensive took the Entente troops by surprise. With the courage of despair, the German units attacked. Seventy divisions from the east had strengthened their own ranks. Berlin knew it was make or break. The unrestricted submarine war had drawn the USA into the war and 100,000 fresh troops arrived every month. Time was not ticking in Germany's favour.

The German spring offensive caused a temporary crisis on the Entente side. Only the unified leadership of the French Marshal Ferdinand Foch made it possible to resist the German attack and limit the damage where the front broke down. The battle raged until the autumn

Bela Kun

US President Woodrow-Wilson

of 1918, but there was no real strategic breakthrough. This was the prelude to November 1918, the end of the First World War and the end of the German Empire. With Kaiser Wilhelm II's flight to the Netherlands, the Hohenzollern monarchy collapsed. Georgia could no longer rely on German support against the communists

Lenin

and now hastily sought help from the Entente and especially from the British, who had long been interested in the oil-rich soil (Baku) of the Caucasus.

Georgia shared the fate of other small countries around the superpowers, such as the states of Central Europe, which were always dependent on other states. For Georgia, it was all just a stay of execution. Its triumphant independence was finally smothered in blood when, on 28 February 1921, Bolshevik troops captured Tbilisi after heavy fighting with nationalist student militias. Moscow once again ruled Georgia, to the frustration of the population who had been so emboldened by national sentiments.

Treaty of Brest-Litowsk

Russian Revolution

Tsaar Nicolaas II and his family

Approximation of Moscow and Berlin via Rapallo

Since the Great October Revolution, two basic ideas had been at odds: the global internationalist ambitions of communism/socialism versus the nation state. In the east, these were the superpowers: Soviet Union, that had officially existed since 1922, versus the new German Reich that had risen from the ashes after November 1918. In between were the small powers with Poland as the biggest player and to some extent a regional power.

Germany had withstood the communist Spartakist uprisings with difficulty, but had - partly due to these upheavals - slipped further and further into the authoritarian course that was formally established in 1933, when Adolf Hitler came to power. He had

Adolf Hitler came to power in 1933

seized dictatorial power after the fire in the Reichstag building.

With the arrival of Hitler, the relationship between Nazi Germany and the Soviet Union came under pressure. After the First World War, there had been cooperation between Berlin and Moscow, in addition to the problems of the communist council republics. The basis for this was the Treaty of Rapallo, which had been signed in the Italian seaside resort on 16 April 1922. In that treaty, the creation of the Soviet Union was recognised and the way for cooperation of all kinds was paved. This was beneficial to both regimes, as both Germany and the Soviet Union were international 'pariahs'. The cooperation had also been partly military. With the arrival of Hitler, the situation intensified. The Nuremberg Race Laws and the Nazi focus on the Slavic 'Untermensch' did not help. Also, the geopolitical ideas about 'Lebensraum' (living space that had to be sought in Eastern Europe) and 'Heim ins Reich' (all Germans within one border) caused tensions.

These tensions caused German political attempts to gain influence over the politics of Central and Eastern Europe. The Soviet Union and Nazi Germany would increasingly come to oppose each other.

On the eve of the Second World War, tensions rose enormously. The most turbulent was the clash in Spain. The years between 1936 and 1939 were the years of the Spanish Civil War. Here, an open trial of strength had taken place between the ideologies of fascist countries Italy and Nazi Germany, and the Soviet Union. The

Treaty of Rapallo

countries mentioned experimented a great deal with new weapons techniques and strategies. In the end, General Francisco Franco was victorious, but it had been a gruelling war that left a deep trail of blood.

Ukraine and Pavlo Skoropadsky

Behind the scenes, an intelligence war also raged around the Ukrainian situation. The Ukrainian freedom movement had only been able to profit from the space that the collapse of the Habsburg and Tsarist Empires offered politically and territorially for a very short time. The first steps towards partial self-government took place - under German supervision - under Pavlo Skoropadsky, a regime that relied mainly on large land holdings. But there were internal rumblings in the Ukrainian camp and the opponents of Ukrainian independence were not sitting still. The Ukrainians suffered from the same problem as the Kurds. They were a great nation that had the misfortune to live at the intersection of many cultures. The Austrians, Hungarians, Germans, Russians, Bolsheviks, Romanians and Czechs had it in for their territory. One by one, Ukrainian leaders had to flee abroad because the pursuit of freedom was sabotaged by one of these parties.

The modern history of Ukraine can be divided into a "Sondernweg" for the eastern part and the "Werdegang" for the western part. Politically, the western part of Ukraine was of particular importance to the struggle for freedom. In practice, this western part was not geographically static, but broadly speaking corresponded to the part that did not belong to Russia. Those areas were subject to old claims by other countries. Galicia and Bukovina fell under the Habsburg Empire from 1772 and 1774 respectively. Before that, there were Polish-Lithuanian claims. After 1918, Polish influence in Galicia increased again, as it did in Volhynia. The Romanians encroached on Bessarabia, despite large Ukrainian communities in Khotyn and Bilhorod. The Hungarians reached into Transcarpathia and the Czechoslovaks into Subcarpathia. All this resulted in a permanent tension in the region with asymmetrical civil war-like conflicts. Especially the Polish-Ukrainian tensions were high. There was even an assassination attempt on the Polish statesman Józef Pilsudski at the height of the tensions. Many Ukrainian freedom fighters disappeared into Polish prisons or fled to the West.

Pavlo Skoropadsky

Holodomor, starvation of the Ukraine

In Eastern Ukraine, the situation was even more serious. There the so-called Holodomor took place: the starvation of the area that peaked in the years 1932-1933. The historical debate on this terrible event is still ongoing. It is partly a technocratic discussion about the extent to which the starvation of millions of Ukrainians as well as inhabitants of the Kuban was a planned genocide. As with any complex historical event, there were also 'exculpatory' documents, including one on emergency food aid from Moscow to the region, but the fact remains that the famine was the result of harvests confiscated by the Communists.

Mass graves near Kharkov

Holodomor, starvation of Ukraine

Stalin's aim with this terrible terror was the destruction of the Ukrainian élan to ever achieve 'nation building'. Not only was hunger used as a weapon, but ethnic cleansing was also deployed for this purpose. A well-known story is the policy of Lazar Kaganovich. He was from Ukraine, but turned out to be one of Stalin's cruellest henchmen. During the Russian Revolution, he had played a leading role in Belarus and in the 1920s he had forcibly implemented the Soviet system in Turkestan. In addition, as a bureaucrat and meeting fanatic, he had subjected Stalin's party bureaucracy entirely to the will of the Kremlin. With regard to the Ukrainians, Kaganovich carried out deportations which also affected many Cossacks who were deported 'northwards'. Many Ukrainian towns were then Russified, a downright policy of repression. Especially in Eastern Ukraine, the

The Ukrainian flatlands were kept in line with hunger

traces of this are still noticeable today, for example, the recent tensions between Putin and the regime in Kiev regarding the Donuch-basin.

The debate on the Holodomor that took place in the past between historians such as Robert Conquest and Alec Nove has shifted in recent years around the question of whether the destruction of Ukraine or the small independent farmer in the area was central. The fact is that Stalin's policy served both purposes and they were not mutually exclusive. However one looks at it, this policy led to collectivisation and repopulation. According to the historians Victor Danilov,

R.W. Davies and Stephen G. Wheatcroft, all this resulted in an unprecedented bloodbath, which was what made the Ukrainians receptive to cooperation with Nazi Germany, and why the German troops were welcomed as liberators in large parts of Ukraine.

Murder on the Coolsingel

While mass murders and ethnic cleansing took place, a shadowy espionage and intelligence war was raging elsewhere in the world. For instance, on 23 May 1938, the Ukrainian leader and freedom fighter Yevhen Konovalets fell victim to a bomb attack on the Coolsingel in Rotterdam. He was literally blown to bits. Shortly before, he had met with someone at the Atlanta Hotel. The man presented himself as a fellow Ukrainian fighter, but in reality turned out to be none other than Soviet top spy Pavel Sudoplatov. This was the man who, through Operation 'Duck', would also have Stalin's greatest political rival Leon Trotsky killed in Mexico.

Sudoplatov later wrote his memoir, *Special Tasks*, with his son Anatoli. It is interesting to see how Sudoplatov justified Konovalets' murder. He stated that Konovalets was an ardent Ukrainian nationalist who did not hesitate to fight for the Ukrainian national cause through bomb

Special agent Pavel Sudoplatov

Bombing on the Coolsingel

attacks against Poles and Bolsheviks. But Sudoplatov also revealed that Konovalets was in league with the Nazis and that Ukrainian separatists were susceptible to Nazi ideology. Indeed, the extremely harsh political climate in which the Ukrainian freedom struggle took place was no cradle for democratic development. It was simply a coming and going of hardliners who, to

put it mildly, matched Mussolini's ideological notions. Sudoplatov, however, forgot to mention that the Soviet Union were not particularly innocent either, which became clear when the Red Army entered Poland on 17 September 1939, following the Wehrmacht on 1 September 1939, and occupied the eastern part of that country as part of the Molotov-Ribbentrop Pact, concluded in August of that year. It also occupied Western Ukraine, which was under Polish control.

Yevgen Konovaletsj

Konovaletsj's grave in Rotterdam

Stepan Bandera, "Ehrenhaft" and Operation "Barbarossa

A thin line between realism and ideology

The developments in Ukraine showed that there were diplomatic and political opportunities for Nazi Germany in Eastern Europe. The oppression of the minority peoples in the Soviet Union and Kaganovich's policy of repression had led to enormous antipathy and distrust of Moscow among national elements in the Baltic States, Belarus and Ukraine. As the Wehrmacht moved further east, minorities in the Crimea and the Caucasus followed.

At odds with the enthusiasm of the liberated peoples were the dogmatic 'Ostpolitik' of Berlin and the views of Hitler himself. The racial laws were difficult to combine with the wishes of the Slavic Ukrainians. In addition, Hitler was convinced of a quick victory over the Soviet Union and was reluctant to share the spoils of war. At the same time, Ukrainian nationalists, like other nationalist forces in Central and Eastern Europe, were relatively pro-German, but still primarily focused on their own interests. Hitler was pragmatic in this regard; in Romania, for example, he did not choose the Romanian fascists of Horia Sima, preferring instead leaders who were more moderate with a broader base of support, such as Marshal Ion Antonescu. This led to strange situations. For example, when

Erich Koch

fascist allies were taken into 'Ehrenhaft', a kind of glorified imprisonment.

The same thing happened in Ukraine. In the Moscow-occupied part of Poland, the Galician Ukrainian freedom fighter in the line of Konovalets, Stepan Bande-

Gerhard von Mende

ra, was freed by the Nazis in Lemberg. Bandera was a hardline Ukrainian nationalist who was imprisoned in part for the planned murder of Polish politician Bronislaw Pieracki. The German invasion of Poland led to his liberation and immediately sparked a new wave of Ukrainian separatism. Bandera and his supporters within the Organisation of Ukrainian Nationalists (the OUN) were valued by the Nazis for their anti-Communist sympathies, but when he declared Ukrainian independence Berlin turned against him. Bandera disappeared in captivity and was transferred to KZ Sachsenhausen, where other prominent prisoners were also held. Berlin kept Bandera in 'reserve' and would bring out this Ukrainian nationalism again when the Red Army advanced further west after the battle of Stalingrad.

On the eve of the German invasion of the Soviet Union, the first 'Osttruppen' were formed. In other words, citizens of the Soviet Union who were recruited for the German army. Initially, these were special units for commando actions, often in enemy uniform, to be able to take bridges and the like by surprise. The capture of a strategic bridge saved a lot of time for the invading German troops.

Under the command of Wilhelm Carnaris, the German intelligence service 'Abwehr' had set up units of Soviet citizens in German service. This happened in April 1941, just before operation 'Barbarossa' within the so-called 'Legion of Ukrainian Nationalists'. This was divided into two specific units, 'Sondergruppe Nachtigall' and 'Organisation Roland'. These units were in turn assigned to the German command of the unit 'Brandenburg-800' and were deployed in cooperation with the German 1. Gebirgsdivision, in the surroundings of Lemberg, where many of the volunteers came from. In the so-called 'Sonderkommando PuMa', members of the Ukrainian nationalist movement OUN-M were recruited to help the Nazis with local administration and government immediately after the Soviet invasion. Thus, unlike 'Nagtigall' and 'Roland', it was not the intention that 'PuMa' would be at the front, but that they would be a support for the German occupation force of Ukraine, 'the Reichskommissar in Reichskommissariat Ukraine', Erich Koch, the former 'Gauleiter' of East Prussia, a double function

KZ Sachsenhausen

Stepan Bandera

that he combined with 'Chef der Zivilverwaltung' of the Bialystok district.

This is where the first problems arose. The intellectual framework of PuMa admittedly had an excellent knowledge of German, and in that sense were an excellent intermediary between the German occupiers. However, at the same time, they were loyal to the Ukrainian ideals. Just as the Germans initially considered Bandera an ally, distrust soon set in. How reliable were these new allies to Berlin? Reports soon reached the German capital that people were working on the Ukrainian cause under the German cover. There was nothing to do but dissolve PuMa.

This debacle was the prelude to the awkward split between National Socialism, Ukrainian particularism and the reality of war. The German civil service was quick to identify the obvious opportunities. But here, too, it was a thin line between realism and ideology, alongside the enormous competition between the various organisations and ministries, defence and the SS. All had their own agenda, and Hitler ruled over them by decree. Nevertheless, as early as 30 June 1941, the German Foreign Ministry met to briefly discuss the initial findings. The German attack on the Soviet Union, 22 June 1941, was only eight days old. The focus was on the practical recruitment of Soviet citizens for the German armed forces, including both the army and the Waffen-SS, the armed wing of Heinrich Himmler's SS empire. One of the contributors was the Turkestan specialist, Professor Gerhard von Mende, who pointed out that there were opportunities to recruit (Islamic) volunteers among the rapidly growing number of prisoners of war that the Wehrmacht was taking from the Red Army. The Islamic peoples were just like the Christian Caucasian peoples, in that they had suffered greatly under Stalinism. The Marxist ideology had hardly any room for religion, which was very important for the Caucasian peoples. Here too, as with Ukraine, there was some preparation. It was

Wilhelm Canaris

not for nothing that the diplomatic post in Turkey had been assigned to the prominent politician diplomat Franz von Papen. This aristocrat was, despite the fact that he had lost several friends in the "Night of the long knives" in 1934, still dedicated to the German cause in Turkey. Moreover, he was stationed in Turkey during the First World War. Within the pan-Turkish movement, he worked for a pro-German course, as a response to anti-colonial and especially anti-German sentiments in the Middle East. But he also fought against the Soviet subjugation of the Turkish peoples in the east, whereby one could fall back on anti-Russian sentiments from the Crimean War of 1853-1856 as well as the Turkish-Russian War of 1877-1878. Thus, there were secret German contacts from an early stage, partly via Turkey, with the Crimean Tatars. They would not do the Germans any harm. During the conquest and occupation of the Crimea in 1941-1942, the Crimean Tatars would be very cooperative. Normally, recruited 'Osttruppen' were taken to Poland for observation and training, but the Crimean Tatars were immediately given a weapon and joined the fight. They were especially important in the fight against the partisans, because they knew the local situation. They also provided assistance to the notorious 'Einsatzgruppen' who hunted down Jews and communists.

Establishment of units and militia as of June 1941

The above-mentioned consultation of June 1941 led to the rapid creation of the first armed units from the Soviet peoples. How far the cooperation with representatives of the various minorities went became clear to the Turkmen after two Turkish generals, through the mediation of the German ambassador Von Papen, visited German prisoner-of-war camps to see whether recruiting Turkmen volunteers was possible. These were Generals Erkilet and Erden. To be on the safe side, the Turkish generals travelled to the German camps as private individuals in order to avoid unintentional diplomatic problems.

Turkmen volunteers

Cossack unit

The arrival of the Turks did indicate that there were serious possibilities. Von Mende then urged the authorities to select prisoners of war by ethnicity and house them. This could speed up the process of targeted recruitment. The specialists of the 'Ostforschung' (Eastern Research) saw other possibilities, which became clear with the formation of Armenian, North Caucasian and Caucasian-Islamic legions in December 1941, in addition to the Turkestans. Not much later, a unit for Azerbaijani volunteers was formed, followed by a Wolgatarian legion in the course of 1942. Von Mende's plan for separate prison camps was inplemented to a degree and strengthened the recruitment drive.

How far-reaching fantasy of the Foreign Office was also shown by the creation of the so-called 'Sonderstab Felmy' under the leadership of General Hellmuth

German anti-aircraft guns in action in the Caucasus

Felmy, who tried to win Arab volunteers for German military service in North Africa and elsewhere. This led to the establishment of the so-called 'Deutsch-Arabische-Lehrabteilung', the DAL.

It was very ad hoc, and organisations and responsibilities changed rapidly. Out of the DAL came the so-called Arab Legion, but the number of recruits was not great.

In Ukraine, things did not go as planned either. Besides Bandera, the Nazis had also arrested Yaroslav Stetsko. He had been the temporary head of the Ukrainian independence proclaimed by Bandera, which was the reason the Germans arrested him. Stetsko was from Tarnopol, formerly part of the Austro-Hungarian Empire, and had previously clashed with the Polish authorities. Following his and Bandera's arrest, Ukrainian leaders met, again at the Atlanta Hotel in Rotterdam, to discuss the case. But it soon became apparent that Berlin's hands were tied. There was little room to manoeuvre, even if it was more than under Stalin. The shared anti-Semitism was but a mere 'consolation'.

The German occupiers, meanwhile, struggled with their own ideological limitations. The divided area in the east fell under the Wehrmacht - Korpsrückwärts (Korück) and then passed into the 'Zivilverwaltung'. Amidst the disputes between sound reason and party doctrine was the fate and role of the 'Volksdeutschen', ethnic Germans who lived among the 'Ostvölker'. It was rather difficult for German politics to determine who exactly could claim this status, if they wanted it at all. Being a Volksdeutscher often meant militarisation of one's existence, such as Volkswehren, service in the Wehrmacht or Waffen-SS, and not infrequently one became part of a population policy resulting in repopulation.

There was also disagreement about the definition of the term 'Volksdeutscher'. In order to put clearify this confusion, the OKW (Oberkommando der Wehrmacht) finally came up with a concrete definition on 15 July 1941, followed by an instruction on how these people should be treated. The latter was

Cossack in German military service

The Polka performed in Wehrmacht uniform

Young Cossack

no unnecessary luxury given the fact that murder and mayhem were rife in the newly occupied territories. The OKW followed the guidelines of the Hauptamt Volksdeutsche Mittelstelle, the VoMi, an organisation led by SS-Obergruppenführer Werner Lorenz, which represented the interests of the Volksdeutschen. VoMi was founded in 1937 and increasingly focused on the situation in Eastern Europe.

Osttruppen in Trawniki and elsewhere

In addition to the initial recruitment of volunteers through the various legions, the SS training centre Trawniki was also used to train 'Osttruppen', the collective term for volunteers from the Soviet Union, from 17 July 1941. The initiative came from the SS-Hauptamt and was put on the map in the Polish town of Trawniki via the offices of Himmler's confidant, the Austrian SS Odilo Globocnik. Globocnik appointed Karl Streibel, an SS officer from Sturm Bann Füher, who then trained the men to become 'Wachmanschaften' for the SS. Streibel would continue to do this work until the camp was evacuated in July 1944.

Trawniki was only the drop in the ocean regarding this very dark side of collaboration. Anyone who reads the reports of the Einsatzgruppen, who went around killing behind the front and regularly found collaborating units and militias helping the SD

Soldier of the Osttruppen with decorations

The Osttruppen were recruited from prisoner-of-war camps. Photo shows captured soldiers of the Red Army in the Crimea

and SS murderers, will find that this was only a drop in the ocean.

Meanwhile, military collaboration was growing rapidly. Until December 1941, the German advance was proceeding smoothly and enormous numbers of Soviet soldiers fell into German hands. These soldiers were taken captive under the worst imaginable conditions, to ensure that German service soon offered a tempting way out. There were also many defectors. One of the most talked-about examples was the defection of an entire Russian regiment led by Major Kononow (regiment 436 of the 155ste division) in August 1941. In September 1941 initiatives were taken within the supreme command of

Turkmen volunteers

Heeresgruppe Mitte (the army group Middle), where in talks between staff officers Henning von Tresckow and Major Freiherr von Gersdorff a decision was made to recruit 200,000 Russian volunteers, to support the Wehrmacht. The plans were submitted by staff officer Hauptmann Strik-Strikfeldt in a 'Denkschrift' (memoir) to Marshal Walther Heinrich Alfred Hermann von Brauchitsch, commander of the OKH (Oberkommando des Heeres). Brauchitsch, who was also in direct contact with Hitler, immediately saw the importance of this initiative and wrote in the margin: 'I see this as decisive for the war'.

'I see this as decisive for the war.'

The cat was out of the bag. They needed the help of the people of the Soviet Union to win the war. Up until then, the German army had never had to fight for more than six weeks at a stretch. However, the scale and scope of the campaign in Russia was unprecedented. In December 1941, the attack on Moscow came to a standstill. In the 'Winterstellung' the Wehrmacht struggled to hold out, and the losses and disappointment were enormous. The 'Russification' of the East Field operation had to be given greater priority, according to many.

German Wehrmacht in the Crimea

Otto Ohlendorf

By the end of 1941, all kinds of initiatives had already been taken, such as the formation of six Crimean battalions. The battle for the Crimea had broken out in all its intensity. Sebastopol was a strategic Black Sea port and from the Crimea the Soviets could reach the strategic Romanian oil fields near Ploesti. The conquest of the Crimea was thus of great importance, and one of Hitler's most capable officers, Field Marshal General and key strategist Erich von Manstein, was in command. The Crimean Tatars, serving under the notorious Einsatzgruppe D, supported the German plans. Einsatzgruppe D was commanded by notorious commander

German troops enter Sebastopol

Citizens deported by Stalin

Dr. Otto Ohlendorf, later succeeded by Walter Bierkap, and was responsible for the murder of many thousands of Jews and Communists.

Theodor Oberländer

Besides the "Denkschrift" of Heeresgruppe Mitte being pulished, the "Denkschrift" *Deutschland und der Kaukasus* by the Meiningen-born politician/thinker Theodor Oberländer also appeared. Oberländer combined 'Realpolitik' concerning the 'Osttruppen' with his insights on Caucasian collaboration and Nazi ideology. For example, he had previously developed a plan to win the Polish for Nazi Germany by allowing them to share in the large Jewish 'loot' in Poland. With regard to his 'Denkschrift' of October 1941, he described the geography of the Caucasus, the influence of Bolshevism on the region and the German opportunities in the Caucasus, in which Oberländer mainly referred to religious freedom for the (Islamic) peoples and the restitution of land as an anti-collectivisation policy.

The initiatives of Heeresgruppe Mitte and Oberländer's 'Denkschrift' led to scepticism from Hitler's immediate circle. Marshal Wilhelm Keitel, a direct confidant of Hitler, increasingly criticised the army's political interference in matters on the Eastern Front. It was clear that Keitel considered this to be beyond the competence and command structure of the armed forces. His criticism was therefore mainly aimed at Heeresgruppe Mitte. "'These matters are none of the Heeresgruppe's business,' he said. 'This is not a matter

Theodor Oberländer

of discussion for the Führer'". This issue, as well as tensions due to the disappointing results of operation 'Barbarossa' led to the removal of Von Brauchitsch and General Von Bock, who supported the plans for collaboration, at the end of 1941.

The fate of German-Russian cooperation seemed to have been sealed, but it was not. There was simply another reality alongside the reality in the Führer's headquarters. There, from the policy of Lebensraum and the elaboration of the 'Generalplan Ost', a radical revolutionary programme emerged. But these plans were disconnected from the reality of the front. The defeat of Moscow raised questions about the outcome of the war. On 23 November, Franz Halder, Chief of Staff of the Army, already noted that the complete destruction of the Soviet forces in 1941 was an illusion, and that one therefore had to prepare for a long war, with all its consequences. Halder noted his fearful suspicion of the future; he saw the Soviet Union as an 'infinite space', hardly conquerable and with 'inexhaustible resources'.

Amin el Husseini

The advocates of cooperation with the Soviet peoples had gained an unexpected ally. On 28 November 1941, the Grand Mufti from Jerusalem had arrived in Berlin. Hadji Mohammed Amin el Husseini. This radical figure considered himself a fervent opponent of Jewry and Zionism and saw an ally in Nazi Germany. He supported radical radio broadcasts from Nazi Germany to the Middle East. He urged Hermann Göring, Hitler's Luftwaffe chief, to bomb Jewish quarters in Palestine. For the Nazis, Husseini was an Arab ally, and useful as a fellow combatant on both the Western and Eastern Fronts. He wanted to support the Germans in recruiting Islamic volunteers.

Amin el Husseini visiting the Waffen-SS unit "Handschar" at the front in Yugoslavia

The development of the units was meanwhile more or less going on under the radar of the Führer headquarters. One could speak of a condoned construction of sorts. This may sound strange in the Führer state, but internally the Third Reich had its own dialectic. Dual functions and overlapping authorities fought each other. This gave Hitler absolute power by proxy.

Target practice

By early 1942, no less than 150 battalions of Osttruppen had been raised. About 70 battalions of these consisted of Ukrainian volunteers, the rest of Belarusians, Balts, Crimean Tatars and Caucasian peoples. In addition, there was an incalculable jumble of smaller militias and units which, in Ukraine for example, were assigned to the 'Hilfspolizei' or the 'Hilfswachmanschaften'.

After Heeresgruppe Mitte came up with initiatives in 1941, Heeresgruppe Süd followed closely behind. On 4 January 1942, it was reported that several Tatar units had again been formed. These volunteers were also used for propaganda purposes against Soviet divisions in the Crimea. Through loudspeakers and leaflets, they tried to get Caucasian Soviet soldiers to defect. A battle for the 'Hearts and Minds' was going on under the suspicious eye of the Führer headquarters. The propaganda had oppor-

El Husseini was deployed to mobilise Islamic volunteers

tunities. On 7 January 1942, for example, the intelligence service of the German 16th I.D. reported that the Caucasian troops of the Red Army facing them had remarkably low morale. Moscow's Soviet oppression and anti-Islamic attitude had caused much ill blood. Defections were a daily occurrence.

The Wehrmacht itself worked continuously to professionalise its cooperation with the Osttruppen. On 9 January 1941, the 'Merkblatt für die Behandlung der Tataren' was drawn up, followed on 2 June 1942 by a 'Denkschrift' on 'Turkvölker'. Hitler himself also showed some flexibility, after he agreed to set up an "Arab Legion" following Husseini's visit. In addition, an office for the Grossmoefti El Husseini, the so-called 'Arab Bureau', was opened in Berlin. Immediately after Hitler's decision, on 13 January, the 'Turkestanian Legion' and the 'Caucasian-Mohammedanian Legion' were founded.

Murderous Ukrainian militias

The need for Osttruppen was growing. One of the men actively recruiting for the army was Claus Schenk Graf von Stauffenberg. He was also the man responsible for the failed attempt on Hitler on 20 June 1944. Regarding the participation of the Osttruppen, he pointed out in a lengthy letter of 15 January 1942 that the participation of the 'Ostvölker' was important for the formation of the 'Schicksalgemeinschaft' Europe.

That there were still a few things wrong with this 'community' became clear from the fact that in the slibstream of militarisation old accounts of eastern volunteers were settled. Ukraine wrote bloody history again in the process. Between June 1941 and mid-1942, almost the entire Jewish population of the region was murdered. From the Nazi point of view, the Soviet Union was a product of 'Jewish-Bolshevism', and mass executions of Jews and communists with Ukrainian help were the result. But the violence did not stop there. The Ukrainian 'Wachmanschaften' also left a huge blood trail through the Ukrainian country, targeting other population groups, especially the Polish. Armed Ukrainian nationalists, the UPA, went on a killing spree through Wolhynia. The killing continued there until March 1943 and then moved to eastern Galicia. There had always been relatively much violence in the region, but now doz-

Einsatzgruppen in action

ens of villages were systematically massacred. The Germans were at a loss; the UPA was a good force against emerging communist partisans, but operated wildly and uncontrollably, without German direction. In practice, they were also targeting the German occupier. The Polish again sought refuge in German auxiliary police battalions, and these Polish then turned against Ukrainian villages. It had become a madness of 'Alle gegen Alle'. According to the historian Grzegorz Rossolinski Liebe, many tens of thousands of people lost their lives.

Constructions of tolerance, arbitrariness and impotence now alternated, while the contribution of the Soviet collaboration increased. This concerned not only armed legions and battalions, but also the so-called Hilfswilligen (Hiwis), who at first did not even 'exist' officially, but who became more and more a

Claus Schenk, von Stauffenberg

permanent part of the German units. They did hand-me-downs, such as the job of driver and took care of logistics. In autumn 1942, 200,000 Hiwis served in the German army. By spring 1943, the number had reached 310,000. Thus, 10% of the German field army were Hiwi.

This is a little known fact, but not so surprising when one considers that Germany at the height of its power had 60 to 70 million Soviet inhabitants living in occupied territory. The importance of cooperation was underlined by a plea from Reinhard Gehlen, the foreman of the German military intelligence in the east, the 'Abteilung Fremde Heere Ost'. Gehlen, too, believed that cooperation was inevitable and the only solution to bring Operation 'Barbarossa' to a successful conclusion.

This advice was taken to heart during Operation 'Blau', the German attack plan for the summer of 1942. The German troops would not only advance towards the Volga, but also with Heeresgruppe A into the Caucasus. This would provide a new and direct contact with the peoples there, who were sceptical about Moscow, to say the least. Weisung No. 41 was announced on 5 April 1942, and after the repulsion of a Soviet offensive near Kharkov, May 1942, under the command of Soviet Marshal Semyan Tymoshenko, the operation started.

While the German tanks rolled towards Kuban and the Volga, the German hinterland was called upon again for the Endsieg. In the *deutsche Ukraine Zeitung* from those days there are numerous reports about the mobilisation of Ukrainian workers for the German cause around the ore area and coal basin of Donetsk and Melitopol. The mines in the strategic region had been systematically destroyed by the Soviets as part of the 'scorched earth' campaign. There was much and heavy work to be done, which was time consuming.

The discovery of Andrei Vlassov

But in the midst of all the adversity there was a moment of hope, which was when Major General Tresckow and other pro-collaboration forces suddenly had the Russian general Andrei Vlassov in their sights. Born in Lomakino in 1901, Vlassov was one of the best generals in the Red Army. He had been selected by the Soviet Stavka to assist in the liberation of surrounded Leningrad. The population there suffered greatly under the German siege. Soviet troops tried to break through the front of the German Heeresgruppe Nord at the Wolchov, at the Ilmensee (Staraja Russa) and more south at Cholm. It was an enormous test of strength and little ground was gained. The swampy, wooded ground made coordination of the battle very difficult. It was a war of positions. Nevertheless, Stalin wanted results and thus ensued endless attacks with terrible losses. Vlassov had to force a breakthrough and he was sent in the 'Kessel'. Soviet troops who had wanted to encircle Leningrad were themselves surrounded by the Germans. This meant the end of Vlassov's career in the Red Army. The encircled Soviet army could not be saved and after an exhaustive battle, Vlassov was taken prisoner.

Tresckow recognised the possibilities that this situation offered. In consultation with Von Stauffenberg and General Ernst-August Köstring, who had taken on a coordi-

General Andrei Vlassov

Vlassov and staff officers

nating function with regard to the Osttruppen, he decided to approach Vlassov. After his capture, Vlassov was taken to the fortress of Lötzen, where valuable prisoners were always interrogated. A few days later, he was put on a plane to Winniza, where the Führer headquarters and the headquarters of the German military high command, the Oberkommando der Wehrmacht (OKW), were located. There, Vlassov was put in a 'Sonderlager'.

Having calmed down here, Vlassov proved receptive to cooperation. On 3 August 1942, he drafted a 'Denkschrift' on the future of Russia. Together with other prominent Russian prisoners, such as commander Vladimir Boyarsky, Vlassov expressed the wish to cooperate with the Germans as 'allies of equal standing'.

Vlassov's declaration was of enormous historical value to Nazi Germany. In addition to the Ukrainians and the Caucasian peoples, this was the ultimate opportunity to win over the anti-Communist Grand Russians. The wind seemed to be in the sails. The *Deutsche Ukraine Zeitung*, meanwhile, brought news of agricultural anti-collectivist land policy east of the Dnieper River on 18 August 1942. This was the way to get a broad coalition. In Winniza, just outside the Führer's bunker and away from Hitler, planning, thinking, weighing and weighing took place. Meanwhile, since September 1942, some 800,000 to 900,000 Soviet citizens had been under German arms. All without official permission from Hitler, possibly even without his knowledge of the numbers. The new Vlassov initiative could be the deciding factor. It was no coincidence that Theodor Oberländer published his second 'Denkschrift' in those days, in which he again advocated the further exploitation of German interests in the Ukraine.

Opportunities in the Kalmücken-steppe

Hardly a month later, on 14 October 1942, a German 'Erkundigungsfahrt' started in the Kalmücker Steppe. Under the leadership of the Sudeten German Alfred Karasek-Langer, the nomadic steppe people of the Kalmücken were asked to participate in the crusade against Bolshevism. The Kalmücken were receptive to cooperation and were prepared for German service through the 162ste German I.D. For optimists, this was like light at the end of a dark tunnel. But here too, there was a tense alliance between those institutions that sought cooperation and those forces in the German spectrum that wanted to exploit the Kalmücken for the benefit of Germany. The 'Wirtschaftskommando z.b.V. 8' and

Kalmück volunteers, right on photo

Kalmück, drawn by the famous artist Repin

Feldpostbrief Weihnachten 1943

other agencies had intruded the steppe area and were searching for anything of value. There was little industry in the area, but large herds were spotted. These were mainly sheep. The Red Army had been unable to remove some of the herds of cattle, and they were wandering around the country unattended. Professor Von Mende pointed out that there were opportunities here: the Kalmücken would most likely agree to fight for Germany if they were given their freedom. The 'Ostministerium' (Rosenberg) and the military authorities (4th Pz.Armee) also shared the

Kalmück cavalry man

opinion that the collectivised land should be returned to the inhabitants. At the same time, Oberländer published two more "Denkschriften" that pointed to "historical opportunities" in the conquered areas.

Oberländer constables massacres in Taman

In spite of growing insight and sometimes also constructive plans, the basis of all this, cast in the National Socialist ideology, remained very shaky. Oberländer himself was the one who personally experienced this. To his great dismay, he saw the cruel working methods of German soldiers and occupying authorities causing irreparable damage to the fragile mutual trust. For example, on the road from Salawi-Janskaya to Temrjuk, on the Taman peninsula at the foot of the Caucasus, he and his unit 'Bergmann', consisting of Osttruppen, came across long lines of Soviet prisoners. These were transported on a foot march to the Durchgangslager (Dulag) No. 183. Along the route he found at least 200 corpses of exhausted prisoners who had been shot to death by their German guards. The horror of their fellow prisoners and the civilians in the area was great. The residents understandably concluded that there was apparently little difference between Hitler and Stalin.

Oberländer wrote irritated letters, but could not easily change this tradition of the German army. In this is how the system was devouring itself from the inside. This internal rotting process was reinforced by painful developments at the front: operation 'Blau' had brought the German Heeresgruppe Süd to the Volga, but the Red Army stubbornly held out on the banks of the Volga at Stalingrad, and the German 6th army under General Paulus was slowly eroding as its long flanks were being closed in by on coalition forces from Hungary, Romania and Italy.

The long flanks, defended by weak allies, offered the Red Army a unique opportunity. The front lines were broken and by November 1942 Stalingrad was surrounded. German attempts to withdraw from Kotelnikovo with three tank divisions and Romanian infantry failed miserably. In January/February 1943 Paul's 6th army went down in the 'Kessel'. A few thousand Hiwis shared the fate of the German soldiers in the city. For them, there was no mercy.

Stalingrad offers Vlassov chances

As with every setback, the Germans became a little more forthcoming towards their Slavic allies. Vlassov, in the battle damage of Stalingrad, was given space to present his plans in the so-called Proclamation of Smolensk. From this, German-Slavic cooperation was propagated and distributed via millions of flyers on the fronts. Vlassov left for the front to spread propaganda from behind his own lines. To this end, on 25 February 1943, Vlassov was picked up from Berlin to join Heeresgruppe Mitte.

Vlassov's efforts notwithstanding, the Germans became increasingly pessimistic about their chances. An internal German report of 26 April 1943 spoke openly

Ruined city of Stalingrad

Почему я стал на путь борьбы с большевизмом

(Открытое письмо генерал-лейтенанта А. А. Власова)

Призывая всех русских людей подниматься на борьбу против Сталина и его клики, за построение Новой России без большевиков и капиталистов, я считаю своим долгом объяснить свои действия.

Меня ничем не обидела советская власть. Я — сын крестьянина, родился в Нижегородской губернии, учился на гроши, добился высшего образования. Я принял народную революцию, вступил в ряды Красной Армии для борьбы за землю для крестьян, за лучшую жизнь для рабочего, за светлое будущее Русского народа. С тех пор моя жизнь была неразрывно связана с жизнью Красной Армии. 24 года непрерывно я прослужил в ее рядах. Я прошел путь от рядового бойца до командующего армией и заместителя командующего фронтом. Я командовал ротой, батальоном, полком, дивизией, корпусом. Я был награжден орденами Ленина, «Красного Знамени» и медалью «XX лет РККА». С 1930 года я был членом ВКП(б).

И вот теперь я выступаю на борьбу против большевизма и зову за собой весь народ, сыном которого я являюсь.

Почему? Этот вопрос возникает у каждого, кто почитает мое обращение, и на него я должен дать честный ответ. В годы гражданской войны я сражался в рядах Красной Армии потому, что я верил, что революция даст русскому народу землю, свободу и счастье.

Будучи командиром Красной Армии, я жил среди бойцов и командиров — русских рабочих, крестьян, интеллигенции, одетых в серые шинели. Я знал их мысли, их думы, их работы и тяготы. Я не порывал связи с семьей, с моей деревней и знал, чем и как живет крестьянин.

И вот я увидел, что ничего из того, за что боролся Русский народ в годы гражданской войны, он в результате победы большевиков не получил.

Я видел, как тяжело жилось русскому рабочему, как крестьянин был загнан насильно в колхозы, как миллионы русских людей исчезали, арестованные без суда и следствия. Я видел, что растаптывалось все русское, что на руководящие посты в стране, как и в командные посты в Красной Армии, выдвигались подхалимы, люди, которым не были дороги интересы русского народа.

Система комиссаров разлагала Красную Армию. Безответственность, слежка, шпионаж делали командира игрушкой в руках «партийных» чиновников в гражданском костюме или военной форме.

С 1938 по 1939 г. я находился в Китае в качестве военного советника Чан-Кай-Ши. Когда я вернулся в СССР, оказалось, что за это время высший командный состав Красной Армии был без всякого повода уничтожен по приказу Сталина. Многие и многие тысячи лучших командиров, включая маршалов, были арестованы и расстреляны, либо заключены в концентрационные лагеря и навеки исчезли. Террор распространился не только на армию, но и на весь народ. Не было семьи, которая так или иначе избежала этой участи. Армия была ослаблена, запуганный народ с ужасом смотрел в будущее, ожидая подготовляемой Сталиным войны.

Поняв какие огромные жертвы, которые в этой войне неизбежно придется нести русскому народу, я стремился сделать все от меня зависящее для усиления Красной Армии. 99-я дивизия, которой я командовал, была признана лучшей в Красной Армии. Работой и постоянной заботой о порученной мне воинской части я старался заглушить чувство возмущения поступками Сталина и его клики.

И вот разразилась война. Она застала меня на посту командира 4 мех. корпуса.

Как солдат и как сын своей Родины, я считал себя обязанным честно выполнить свой долг.

Мой корпус в Перемышле и Львове принял на себя удар, выдержал его и был готов перейти в наступление, но мои предложения были отвергнуты. Нерешительное, разваленное комиссарским контролем и растерянное управление фронтом привело Красную Армию к ряду тяжелых поражений.

Я отводил войска к Киеву. Там я принял командование 37-ой армией и трудный пост начальника гарнизона города Киева.

Я видел, что война проигрывается по двум причинам: из-за нежелания русского народа защищать большевистскую власть и созданную системой насилия и из-за безответственного руководства армией, вмешательства в ее действия больших и малых комиссаров.

В трудных условиях моя армия справилась с обороной Киева и два месяца успешно защищала столицу Украины. Однако, неизлечимые болезни Красной Армии сделали свое дело. Фронт был прорван на участке соседних армий. Киев был окружен. По приказу верховного командования я был должен оставить укрепленный район.

После выхода из окружения я был назначен заместителем командующего юго-западным направлением и затем командующим 20-й армией. Формировать 20-ю армию приходилось в труднейших условиях, когда решалась судьба Москвы. Я делал все от меня зависящее для обороны столицы страны. 20-я армия остановила наступление на Москву и затем сама перешла в наступление. Она прорвала фронт Германской армии, взяла Солнечногорск, Волоколамск, Шаховскую, Середу и др., обеспечила переход в наступление по всему Московскому участку фронта, подошла к Гжатску.

Во время решающих боев за Москву, я видел, что тыл помогал фронту, но, как и боец на фронте, каждый рабочий, каждый житель в тылу

делал это лишь потому, что считал, что он защищает Родину.

Ради Родины он терпел неимоверные страдания, жертвовал всем. И не раз я отгонял от себя постоянно встававший вопрос:

да полно, Родину ли я защищаю, за Родину ли я посылаю на смерть людей? Не за большевиков ли, маскирующихся святым именем Родины, проливает кровь Русский народ?...

Я был назначен заместителем командующего Волховским фронтом и командующим 2-й ударной армией. Пожалуй, нигде так не сказалось пренебрежение Сталина к жизни русских людей, как на практике 2-й ударной армии. Управление этой армией было централизованно сосредоточено в руках Главного Штаба. О ее действительном положении никто не знал и им не интересовался. Один приказ командования противоречил другому. Армия была обречена на верную гибель.

Бойцы и командиры неделями получали 100 и даже 50 грамм сухарей в день. Они опухали

Smolensk speech by Vlassov

about the fact that 'the Vlassov card' had simply been played too late. The morale of Soviet volunteers on the German side also faltered. As stated in the report, morale depended on the quality of the German commander, and not every officer was suitable for the task. According to a report drawn up by the 'Gruppe Wagner', Brigade Staff 18, the volunteers were only with the Germans because in the Red Army 'it was even worse'. Reports of theft, drunkenness and desertion increased.

The summer of 1943 was of great importance to Nazi Germany. In general, it was the Germans who were on the offensive in the summer and the Russians in the winter. Hitler concentrated his troops for operation 'Zitadelle' which was aimed at the large Soviet front arc around the city of Kursk. In this area Stalin had concentrated 40% of his field army. This offered the German strategists an enormous opportunity. The generals were summoned to Hitler's house and he impressed upon them the importance

Battle of Kursk 1943

Volunteers from the 'Handschar' division

of the coming battle. In cooperation with this, a major propaganda offensive started, operation 'Silberstreif'.

This operation was entirely in the light of the worrying war situation. Not only were things tense around 'Zitadelle', but the Fremde Heere Ost had also issued a warning report on the Soviet war economy. All fronts now faced danger. Silberstreif' was a propaganda campaign directly at the front and the Vlassov initiative played a central role in it. Under the leadership of Oberst Krause and Major Dr. Schäfer, these plans were worked out. Vlassov had to offer a 'Russian' alternative to Stalin. Zitadelle' had to move the military maps, and the newly discovered mass graves near Katyn were used as propaganda. In these forests near Smolensk, thousands of Polish officers had been murdered by Stalin, and the Germans had found these mass graves. The international press was called in to prove the criminal character of the Kremlin regime. Stalin denied with all his might, which would continue until the Yeltsin-Gorbachev era.

The new mobilisations on all fronts in the occupied territory of the Soviet Union were also echoed in other parts of the territory occupied by Nazi Germany. In Bosnia, the German authorities now played on the anti-communist sentiments of the Islamists there. On 4 May 1943, the so-called 'Winkler Report' was drawn up, mapping the 'political layers' of the Bosnians. This was to be the first action to recruit Balkan Muslims in addition to the Islamist Caucasians, which would actually happen in the divisions 'Prinz Eugen', 'Handschar', 'KAMA' and other units.

In July and August 1943, the Battle of Kursk took place. It was a huge 'Materialschlacht' in which the Ger-

Tanks of the division 'Totenkopf' near Kursk 1943

mans gained ground, but could not achieve a strategic breakthrough. The ever hesitant Hitler had postponed the attack for a long time and the Soviet intelligence was well informed about the German plans. The climax of the battle took place on the fields near Prokhorovka. The decision was delayed and, when the Western Allies landed on Sicily and Italy became unstable, Hitler was forced to pull his Waffen-SS divisions from the front and send them south in a hurry. Hitler ordered the 'Zitadelle' to be 'temporarily halted', which could not disguise the fact that Germany's chances for 1943 were over.

Handschar' soldier

Vlassov inspects Soviet volunteers in German service

Tiresome road after the fields of Prokhorovka

The setbacks did not help Vlassov's propaganda work. The reality in the field also remained obstinate. For example, there was a warning message from the 15de Luftwaffe Felddivision of 1 June 1943, which warned against the bad treatment of the Soviet citizens. This also made the Hiwis more unreliable. The division's document also advised the troops to keep an eye on the Hiwis and to report any removal of the troops - attempted desertion - immediately.

In the meantime it had also dawned on Hitler and his immediate circle how structural the dependence on the Hibi had become. During a discussion at the Berghof on 8 June 1943, in the presence of Hitler, Keitel and Zeitzler, it was stated that the number of Hibi's amounted to some 220,000 troops at that moment. When Hitler questioned this, Zeitzler remarked, with a rare moment of realism, that in the artillery it would be difficult to remove gunners 4 and 5 because they were Hiwi.

A stenogram of the meeting on 8 June showed that the position of the Soviets and the Vlassov army were also on the agenda. Far too late, the importance of the Soviet collaboration had become a topic of discussion. One of the consequences of the Berghof meeting was that on 15 June 1943, at last, active recruitment was once again taking place in the POW camps. The living conditions in

Hiwis are trained

the camps were so bad that there was a lot of enthusiasm to work as Hiwi. In the meantime, the spiritual care in the 162 (Turk) I.D. was stepped up, giving Islam more room. Theodor Oberlände supported these initiatives in a new Denkschrift. Ralf von Heygendorff, attached to the Osttruppen and the 162 (Turk) I.D. also drafted a new memo on how German officers should approach the Osttruppen: 'über die wehrgeistige Führung der Legionaire'.

After the Berghof meeting, 1943 was characterizedby numerous initiatives, Denkschriften and internal memos aimed at successfully integrating the Osttruppen. The Führer's headquarters still oscillated between a policy of tolerance and internal aversion, which did not make the task any easier. In addition, the slowly returning opportunities at the front exercised a moderating influence on the success of the collaboration.

In July 1943, there were warning reports from the 256 I.D. about the malfunctioning of the Hiwis. The armed

Soviets on the German side were also increasingly tested by the conditions at the front and the increasing partisan activity in the hinterland. The 256 I.D. operated in the area of Potschinok as part of the XVII. corps in July 1943 and the Ost-batalion 229 was severely tested in combat. Meanwhile, the "Wirtschaftsamt" was also "hunting" the Hiwis and Osttruppen. For example, the 2de army selected workers for the 'Eisen und Stahl Programm' in order to free up more German workers for the front. A first experiment was started with Bau-Pi-Batalion 9. While this was going on, the 162 (Turk) I.D. was expanded with a third regiment on 15 August 1943.

For the year 1943, it could be concluded that it was too little and too late, and even half-hearted on the part of the OKW. The tone of the internal reports had become very serious. For instance, a report of 12 September 1943 of the Heeresgruppe Nord simply stated that 'Russia could only be conquered by the Russians!' In practice, they were quoting Vlassov here. Heeresgruppe Nord therefore argued

A proud Hiwi

Hiwis for handicrafts

that the tricolour white-blue-red of old Russia should be given space to mobilise occupied Russia against Moscow.

The final months of 1943 were riddled with good intentions and stubborn reality. There was increasing pressure on the fronts - in the East it went back towards the Dnieper. The Kuban bridgehead was cleared and the Germans in the Crimea were under pressure. The Korück suffered increasingly from sabotage, to which the German leadership retaliated with terror. This put pressure on the German anti-Soviet policy. On 12 October, in particular, the XXXV. army had to take severe measures against the civilian population in the occupied area, due to partisan activities and help from the population. Hostages were taken and executions carried out. The 24 Pz.D. reported desertions of Hiwis serving in the division in November. Soviet propaganda also played a role, as did activities of the Nationalkomitee Freiers Deutschland, a resistance movement made up of captured German soldiers who now worked for the Communist side.

Himmler discovers the possibilities of collaboration

At the beginning of 1944, history of the Osttruppen entered a new phase. The SS had realised that the mobilisation of the Osttruppen was the answer to the problems of the advancing war. As a result, Heinrich Himmler, the Reichsführer-SS, was increasingly fishing in the same pond as the army. The result was aggressive recruitment practices by the Soviet collaborators. This happened in Poland, where SS recruiters stood in front of the Osttruppen training barracks and snatched volunteers for the army. On 7 January 1944, soldiers of Turk battalion 786 were reported to have been picked up by SS recruiters in Warsaw. For the army, these soldiers were suddenly lost and considered deserters, with all the problems that entailed.

Meanwhile, Himmler's SS went full throttle. Prof. Von Mende of the 'Ostministerium' was called in, as well as the Gereral der Osttruppen in Lötzen,

Reichsführer-SS Heinrich Himmler

Vlassov with propaganda minister Joseph Goebbels

Oberstleutnant Herre. At the SS-Hauptamt, Gottlob Berger put pressure on Osttruppen-General Hellmich. This energetic offensive approach on 12 January 1944 led to the plan to set up a 'muselmanische SS-Division' in the Lublin area in Poland. This took place under the supervision of the Höherer SS und Polizieführer SS-Gruppenführer Jacob Sporrenberg. The spirited Sporrenberg was ordered not to be 'deterred by bureaucracy', so, there was urgency. That same day, a name for the new unit rolled out of the hat: 'Neu Turkestan'.

The formation of 'Neu Turkestan' was as hasty as it was chaotic. On 24 May 1944, Himmler, running ahead, decided that the unit should be given divisional status, whereas in reality it had not yet reached that stage. In order to fill the unit quickly, army units, such as Osttruppen unit I/94, were looted. Meanwhile, Himmler's confidant Alfred Erdmann tried to transfer

Crimean units to the SS. On 7 June, barely a month after the divisional status of 'Neu Turkestan', the SS was already discussing army corps status. Specialists such as Mayer-Maden were recruited to develop specific policies for the 'Osttruppen', including the Grand Mufti of Jerusalem, El Husseini. The radical cleric fitted perfectly into the NS concept, with his fervent anti-Semitism. At the Bosnian Waffen-SS division 'Handschar', where Husseini had visited, pamphlets had been handed out with the text that the prophet Mohammed had been poisoned by Jews.

The SS becomes Vlassov's "ally" and the establishment of "Neu Turkestan".

In order to be able to act quickly with regard to the recruitment of mainly Muslim volunteers, the SS now supported all kinds of political initiatives that were positive towards the Caucasian peoples' desire for autonomy. In fact, the SS now followed in Vlassov's footsteps, although the Russian Liberation Army (ROA) was mainly aiming at big-Russian interests. Meanwhile, various SS leaders were tumbling over each other to implement Himmler's new urgent orders. Given that Himmler's wishful thinking was more central than reality, quarrels and frustration were the result. SS-officer Hermann tried to get in Himmler's way by depicting Mayer-Maden as a 'floating type'. Mayer-Maden was a man with a broad horizon, who thought about how Nazi Germany could create an anti-Bolshevik revolt on the southern flank of the Eastern Front. To this end, he travelled far and wide. This got in the way of his practical work, the construction of 'Neu Turkestan'. Hermann, more of a 'Nur Soldat', attacked him on this. Hermann believed that 'Instrument E', by which he meant unity, was more than an idea. With regard to ideas, he believed more in the Gutter Mufti than in Mayer-Maden.

Practical as he was, Hermann informed Himmler in December 1944 that the Islamic Osttruppen needed a

Divisional symbol of the Galician Waffen-SS

Bronislav Kaminski

flag. The designers of the SS immediately went to work. The order was that the colour green of Islam should dominate. The SS also ordered 50 German translations of the Koran. The bill was sent to the SS-Hauptamt.

In January 1945, the "Turkestan" unit began to take shape and grew in number. The troops were now being trained around Krakow, and three battalions were almost ready for deployment. Kyrgyz and Azerbaijani officers led the unit, in addition to a Turkmen officer. In the Trawniki camp, people were working day in and day out. Despite the progress, there were all kinds of disciplinary problems. The Muslim young men did not integrate well into the local population, and young women in particular were harassed. Rapes occurred and caused great tension. In addition, the 'Turkestan' soldiers got involved in smuggling. The head of the SS-Hauptamt, Gottlob Berger, was informed of the excesses and intervened strongly. The unit was disciplined and immediately transported to Juraciski, near Minsk.

Here, the aim was to "regain control" over the 'Neu Turkestan' troops, but in reality they were handed over to SS-Hauptsturmführer Heinz Billig. Billig was a sadistic psychopath who did not hesitate to throw a hand grenade at a volunteer who had forgotten the password. Executions were the order of the day. Desertions were the result.

After these new fiascoes, the local HSSPF, Von Gottberg, intervened. The Osttruppen were immediately placed under the command of the notorious SS officer Dr Oskar Dirlewanger, a harsh and cruel soldier, who had been pre-sanctioned for sex with minors. He had led a band of poachers that Himmler, in a romantic mood, thought would be suitable as an anti-partisan unit. Indeed, Dirlewanger's actions were often effective, but he killed like crazy. Himmler called the atmosphere in the

Kaminski Brigade in Warsaw 1944

REICHSFÜHRER ⚡⚡ HIMMLER
MOTTAR GENERAL VLASSOV

Propaganda magazine 'Signal' reports on meeting between Himmler and Vlassov

unit 'medieval', which the Reichsführer-SS took as a compliment. In August 1944, the 'Dirlewanger' brigade was deployed during the Warsaw Uprising. With the Red Army at the gates of Warsaw, the Polish underground tried to free itself. The Nazis struck back hard. The actions of 'Dirlewanger' were so cruel that SS commander Erich von dem Bach-Zelewski recoiled. However, the overall commander, SS-Gruppenführer Heinz Reinefarth, kept the unit in the field. Dirlewanger's 3000-plus troops, including two Azerbaijani battalions, were indispensable. Dirlewanger's good connections with the SS-Hauptamt kept him in check. Another unit of Osttruppen, the Kaminski unit, had to pay dearly for their obstinate actions. The German authorities ambushed and executed their commander Bronislav Kaminski and his right-hand man Ilya Stavikin. The Polish rebels were blamed.

The crushing of the Warsaw Uprising was only a minor success in a large overall German withdrawal. Parts of the 'Neu Turkestan' unit had not arrived in Warsaw at all due to the chaos, but were stuck on the railway tracks in Hungary. After the Warsaw Upris-

Dr. Oskar Dirlewanger

ing, 'Neu Turkestan' was deployed in Slovakia, where an anti-German uprising had broken out in October 1944. German resistance to this was directed by General Hermann Höfle from Bratislava (Pressburg). The Turkmen now served in the "Dirlewanger" unit and the troops of SS officer Wilhelm Hintersatz, from Brandenburg. Since 1919, Hintersatz was better known as Harun El-Rashid, because he had converted to Islam after serving in Turkey under Otto Liman von Sanders during World War I. Together with the divisions 'Tatra', 'Schill' and 'Horst Wessel', the Slovakian insurgents were soon defeated. They fled into the mountains, leaving 4,000 dead. Subsequently, the unit 'Neu Turkestan' was deployed in Hungary and Lombardy, but there was no real large-scale front deployment. Himmler's SS experiment with the Caucasian peoples was deployed too late to be decisive. In addition, they were mainly in competition with the army, which did not help the overall German military situation.

The division 'Galizien', between war crimes and soldier's courage

Himmler's second task lay in the Ukraine. There, in February 1944, the HSSPF Wilhelm Koppe had given the order that a Kampfgruppe Ukrainian SS was needed immediately for the defence of Eastern Ukraine. In 1943, on command of Governor Dr. Otto Wächter and SS-Oberführer Fritz Freitag, training of Ukrainian SS of what was called the 14. Waffen-Grenadier-Division - that would become the SS Galizische nr. 1 - began. The Germans themselves were amazed at the enthusiasm with which the Ukrainian youth enlisted. There were more applications than soldiers to be placed. In total, some 72,000 volunteers signed up. The unit was led by direct confidants of Reichsführer-SS Heinrich Himmler. Commander Freitag had been a member of Himmler's personal staff, as well as an officer in the 1st SS-brigade (mot.), a unit operating within 'Kommandostab Reichsführer-SS'. This brigade was closely involved with the Einsatzgruppen and responsible for a large series of massacres in the Soviet Union against Jews and Communists.

The divisional staff consisted mainly of German window personnel, with many officers having previously served in 'Nachtigall' and 'Roland' and thus had some experience with Osttruppen. There were

Ukrainian volunteers

several highly controversial officers within the divisional cadre, such as SS-Hauptsturmführer Heinrich Wiens, who had served in Einsatzgruppe D and had blood on his hands, as well as a staff officer of the 'Dirlewanger' unit, SS-Obersturmbannführer Franz Magall. Ukrainian battalion commanders such as SS-Hauptsturmführer Mikhaiklo Brididir and SS-Sturmbannführer Evhen Pobihuschii had made their careers in Schutzmannschaft battalions. One of these battalions, number 204, had performed hand-to-hand combat duties at the Pustkow concentration camp, where Soviet prisoners of war were held and Polish prisoners were put to work, including on the V-missiles. A total of about 15,000 people are said to have lost their lives there.

Ukrainian propaganda for Nazi Germany

The new Waffen-SS unit 'Galizien' first saw action in eastern Galicia. It was mainly directed against partisans and thus a brutal fight, in which war crimes were likely committed. Anders Rudling, in his research published in *The Journal of Slavic Military Studies*, outlined how at Vitsyn, Palikrowny, Malinksa and Czernicy the unit wreaked havoc. This happened around March 1944. On 16 May 1944, after new training time at Neuhammer, the unit was directed to the front of the 4de Pz.leger, as part of the Heeresgruppe Nordukraïne. The unit was deployed some 36 kilometres west of Brody and was soon sucked into the great German retreat westwards. Members of the U.P.A., the Ukrainian Liberation Army, still in civilian clothes, volunteered on the battlefield. The untrained troops proved hopeless in battle and Fritz Freitag sent them home again. The 14de SS-division had fought bravely around the ruins and the Pidhirci castle. The regiments 24 and 30 had suffered heavy losses there. Almost the entire staff of SS regiment 31 was killed near Sasiw. The survivors broke out in a south-westerly direction, after the German 8. Pz.Div. and 20. Pz.Div. forced a break-out here.

According to Soviet historiography, the losses at Brody amounted to 17,000 German-Ukrainian prisoners and about 30,000 dead. The division had been in existence for only 11 months, and over the span of a few days it was completely dispersed and largely destroyed. The Soviet advance could not be stopped by an additional Waffen-SS division. The remnants of the unit that did survive, spent the final days of the war in Slovakia, where they crushed the Slovakian uprising together with 'Dirlewanger', 'Neu Turkestan' and the Waffen Grenadier Division 'Horst Wessel'.

Himmler and his SS volunteers

The historian Jan Korcek discovered that in Slovakia the Ukrainian Waffen-SS was again involved in at least nine different incidents against humanity.

Fritz Freitag, Commander of Galician Waffen-SS Division

Increasing desertion

In addition to the problems within the SS, the Osttruppen were also increasingly under pressure in the regular army. For example, Hitler's staunchest ally on the Eastern Front, Romanian Marshal Ion Antonescu, did not like Osttruppen. Documents show time and time again that conflicts arose between Germans and Romanians over these units. The Romanians were characterised, as Marshal Erich von Manstein stated, by an irrational fear of the great Russia, which was reflected in their attitude towards the Osttruppen. This was troublesome for the Germans, who used these units extensively in the Crimea and later in the Romanian field in cooperation with the German-Romanian front. On the oilfields of Romanian Ploesti, too, Osttruppen and workers were very active. Antonescu demanded that they be replaced by Romanians. The Romanians, in turn, ran away from every Western Allied air attack. The Ukrainian volunteers worked relentlessly, air raid or not.

There were also alarming reports from the 2th army on 6 August 1944. The number of desertions was increasing. It became more and more clear to the Osttruppen that they had bet on the wrong horse. In the report 'Bericht über Abwehrlage bei landseigenen Hilfskräften', Oberst Machter stated that many Osttruppen were becoming increasingly unreliable. As an example, a partisan attack on the railway junction Kliwmbow, 30

Vlassov and Freitag

kilometres north of the Polish capital Warsaw was mentioned. Several Wolgatatarian units had defected to the side of the partisans. They had taken (machine) guns with them. In the night of 24 to 25 July 1944, the same army had taken the 3./Russ. Sich. Btl. also deserted.

Against all odds, the Wehrmacht continued to build up Osttruppen. On 11 October 1944, master units were set up for this purpose, from which front divisions were to emerge. These were the Freiwilligen-Stamm Division in Freiburg, the Freiw. Stamm Rgt. 1 in Neuhammer, the Freiw. Stamm Rgt. 2 in Ohrdruf, the Freiw. (UKR.)

Stamm Rgt. 3 in Grafenwöhr, the Freiw. (Russ.) Stamm Rgt. 4 and in Grafenwöhr, and Rgt. 5 (Cossacks) in Döllersheim. Furthermore, a Turkestan 'Arbeits und Einsatz' battalion served in Neuhammer and a Turkestan officer's training school was set up in Ohrdruf. On 12 October, the imam-training within the Wehrmacht got off the ground. In the so-called 'Mitteilungen' of 19 November 1944, the most important points for the German officers regarding the Osttruppen were once again listed, which was repeated on 3 March 1945 and 25 March 1945. At that time, it was already quite clear that the whole Osttruppen plan had completely failed.

The late triumph of Vlassov in Hradschin Palace

The downfall of the Vlassov army proved this. The German authorities had kept Vlassov small for a long time because certain circles on the German side were afraid that he would develop into a kind of head of state; but the middle way used by the Germans simply did not work. Vlassov's propaganda offensive in Heeresgruppe Mitte had therefore failed and time was running out. Strangely enough, it was the widespread propaganda of the SS that made Vlassov's message more well-known. The SS had a special position within the Third Reich and could sometimes afford things that other agencies shied away from. The SS might have started late with the Osttruppen, but was energetic when it did.

The SS's late insight paved the way for the final development of the Vlassov movement at five minutes to midnight for the Third Reich. While in Berlin, Vlassov was in feverish contact with his subordinates and on 4 November 1944, his confidants Tschekalow, Sherebkov and Meandrov assembled in Prague where preparations were made for Vlassov's political action. Two days later, on 13 November, the 'Sonderzug' arrived with Vlassov and some of his fellow fighters. The fact that a German guard of honour, who was on standby at the station, was inspected by Vlassov showed how times had changed. The German military commander of Prague, Gener-

General Vlassov with Reichsleiter Baldur von Schirach

al Rudolf Toussaint, made his appearance. Vlassov was then received with full honours at the Czernin Palace by SS-Obergruppenführer and Minister of State Karl Hermann Frank. It was 'a belated triumph' for the Russians, as Vlassov's biographer Sven Steenberg rightly noted. Vlassov was accommodated in the Alcrow hotel where a meeting took place with the General der Osttruppen Ernst Köstring and, despite the German's humility, this meeting came to nothing. Up until then, Köstring had done nothing for Vlassov because his position was not recognised. Now that it could be recognised, Köstring was still uncertain due to the "national character" of the Vlassov movement. Although Köstring was still on the fence, this would not stop Vlassov from making his proclamation with great ceremonial on 14^e November in the Spanish Hall of the Hradschin. In this so-called Prague proclamation, Vlassov called for the overthrow of Stalin and spoke out in favour of cooperation with Germany, but also stressed that he supported the Russian national cause. Hermann Frank, SS-Obergruppenführer Werner Karl Otto Lorenz, leader of the interest group for 'Volksdeutschen' (ethnic Germans outside German territory), the so-called Volksdeutsche Mittelstelle (VoMi), as well as other dignitaries and press, were present. In his speech, Lorenz called Vlassov 'Germany's friend and ally'.

The Prague Manifesto was the start of the so-called KONR, the Committee for the Liberation of the Peoples of Russia. The proclamation was printed in a special magazine, the *Wolja Naroda* (Trap), and hundreds of thousands of pamphlets were dropped from German aircrafts behind the Soviet lines and deep into the Soviet Union.

The seed of truth and its fruit.

Looking back, this late initiative is easy to view with scepticism and disbelief, but for Vlassov and his supporters, the anti-Stalin proclamation was a serious matter. 'The seed of truth has been planted and will bear fruit,' Vlassov told his partners. Then, in prisoner-of-war camps, new soldiers were diligently recruited. A special mass for the KONR initiative was held in the Russian cathedral in Berlin.

Vlassov and his officers came up with creative ideas. They wanted to try making contact with Ukrainian nationalists and the troops of the UPA in order to build up resistance behind the Russian lines. This was inspired by the Ukrainian uprising shortly after World War I, where Bolsheviks and Ukrainian militias fought each other to the death. The Germans supported this initiative, and Hauptmann Witzel (pseudonym Kirn) was dropped behind the Soviet lines to establish contact. Witzel reported that the size of the UPA forces was considerable.

In the meantime, Vlassov was also working to expand his army as much as possible. He was well aware that the pact he had with the Nazis was wafer-thin and born of necessity. The stronger he was, the more independent his operation would be. Connections were made with as many Osttruppen as possible, who were scattered across the fronts.

Vlassov with his men

In practical terms, new divisions were now being created. Here, Köstring proved to be productive, as he recruited Oberst Herre, an experienced commander who was stationed with the 323th German Infantry Division in Northern Italy. As his right hand he chose Major Keiling, a highly decorated officer. They were partly responsible for the creation of the first 'Russian' divisions: the 600th and the 650th infantry divisions.

The 600th division was the first division of the Russkaya Oswobodennaya Armija (ROA), the Russian Liberation Army, and was deployed on the 'Truppenübungsplatz' Müsingen. For this unit, troops had been gathered from the newly established 29. Waffen-Grenadier-Division der SS (Russ. Nr.1, the old Kaminski Troops), as well as from various Russian and Ukrainian units who were already serving. This made up regiments 1601, 1602 and 1603. The training of the units would take until February 1945. Division 650, which was set up a little later, had regiments 1651, 1652 and 1653. The line-up took place at Truppenübungsplatz Heuberg, and later the unit was moved to Münsingen.

The attitude of the new units, especially the old Kaminski troops who had previously caused problems in Warsaw, did raise some eyebrows. The Gestapo warned against insubordination, and the Ostministerium of Nazi-ideologist Alfred Rosenberg felt it had been bypassed and did everything possible to obstruct it. For example, diplomat Hilger, the foreign ministry envoy to Vlassov, was put under suspicion by the Ostministerium and accused of 'Bolshevik sympathies'. It seemed that not only Vlassov was being thwarted, but the German authorities were

Truppenübungsplatz Heuberg

ROA soldiers

also turning against each other. Vlassov's support from the powerful Reichsführer-SS Himmler was now convenient.

The 'breeding ground' of Soviet citizens in German hands

While the training of the Vlassov troops in Münsingen was in full swing, the KONR and the German Statistical Office were working together to chart the 'breeding ground' of Soviet citizens in German hands as best they could. The head of the OKH bureau, Oberst Kurt Passow, calculated that there were still millions of Soviet men in German hands. This included 6 to 7 million Ostarbeiter, 1.2 million POWs and about 1 million Hiwis and volunteers, which meant there was a lot of potential. However, financial resources were needed to recruit an army from it. On 17 January 1945 the German Reich struck a financial agreement with the KONR for loans, which were to be repaid after the conquest of Russia. The German-KONR cooperation would not be called perssimistic, considering that the Soviet offensive on the Weichsel had already begun. In Hungary, the siege of Budapest was in full swing and in the west, the Ardennes offensive had failed. Nonetheless, this financial agreement was the only official document between the German Reich and the KONR and therefore held great symbolic importance. In any case, the measures reflected the SS's attitude towards its new allies. 'From now on, whoever hits Russians will go to the KZ,' Himmler reportedly sarcastically remarked when he noticed arrogant reluctance towards the Vlassov initiative. As a result of this development, Vlassov was appointed commander of the Liberation Army, ROA, on 28 January 1945, which meant that for the first time these units were no longer under the OKW, but stood on their own two feet.

General Heinrich Aschenbrenner

In the days that followed, talks between the military training inspectors, the German authorities and ROA alternated. Luftwaffe General Heinrich Aschenbrenner, specially appointed as the German representative to the air units of the Osttruppen, maintained contact with Vlassov's air force delegate, Malzew. As a former air force attaché to the German embassy in Moscow and an experienced diplomat, Aschenbrenner was the right man for the job. During all of this, Vlassov was received in Karinhall, the wooded residence of Luftwaffe chief Hermann Göring, which had been built by Werner March, the same man who had built the Olympic Stadium in Berlin for the 1936 Games.

Vlassov used these contacts to continue to push for the rapid expansion of the forces under his command. Of great importance were the Cossack units, which fought on the German side on several fronts, mainly in Yugoslavia. The Cossacks had an impressive military tradition and also performed excellently on the German side, both as occupation troops against Tito's partisans and against regular troops of the Red Army. Under the inspiring leadership of the illustrious commander Helmuth von Pannwitz, born in Siberia and descended from a Prussian noble family, units had grown into the XV. SS-Cosaken Kav. Corps. The units had initially started as part of the army, but had been taken over by the Waffen-SS. Vlassov's wish to take Von Pannwitz's troops under his wing was also a matter of discussion for the SS. In competition with the army, Himmler, like Vlassov, wanted to grow as much as possible.

Vlassov's headquarters were moved to Karlsbad in the Czech Republic, where the reception was not very friendly. They moved into the hotel 'Richmond', but Gauleiter Konrad Henlein announced that he was 'not amused' and threatened to use 'Volkssturm' to drive the Russians out of the 'Sudetengau'. Old habits die hard.

Nevertheless, on 16 February 1945, the 1st division of the ROA was ready for action. For the occasion, Köstring visited Vlassov to add gravitas to the moment. In his speech, Vlassov referred to his conversation with Himmler, in which the Reichsführer-SS had assured Vlassov that the old problems were in the past, and that a new dawn was rising.

Himmler tests 'his' Russians at the Oder

Himmler's support came at a price. Soon Vlassov received the order to deploy the new division. It was the moment of truth. Himmler had become commander of the Heeresgruppe Weichsel and every soldier was being used. Hitler had his doubts and stated that the future was simple: 'either the division is right or it is wrong', he announced in a staff meeting on 27 January 1945. It would either be a 'regular' division or an 'idiotic' one.

Vlassov was keen to impress. Special shock troops equipped with 'Sturmgewehren' and 'Panzerfäusten', were formed under the command of Oberst Igor Sakharov. On 9 February 1945, the unit was deployed at the seam between two Soviet divisions. In this action, a Soviet battery of anti-tank guns was destroyed. Internal reporting from Heeresgruppe Weichsel stated that the ROA Russians had remarkably good morale and were much more optimistic than the now demoralised German troops. The German troops used Sakharov's energetic troops as a battering ram (Kulak) to advance.

The efforts of the Vlassov troops had not gone unnoticed. Joseph Goebbels, the Nazi Minister of Propaganda, wrote in his diary that the Russians had 'done a great job'. The German General Wilhelm Berlin, commander of the German 227 I.D., had personally come to thank the Russian officers on the battlefield near Wriezen. In their attack, the ROA soldiers had recaptured the town of Neu-Lewin from the Red Army. Himmler was also convinced and informed Hitler on 9 February 1945 that he wanted to 'continuously reinforce the Eastern Front with Russian units'. It was a strange and unthinkable situation.

After the success, the next step was to decide on a strategy. The chief of operations, Oberstleutnant I.G. De Mazière, noted the importance of continuing to train the ROA troops so their deployment would not result in a fiasco. To this end, the 1st ROA Division was transported by rail to Pasewalk, where the unit was encamped in the hinterland of Von Manteuffel's 3. Here, the troops had guard duties and were further trained.

In mid-March, under the code name 'Verteidigung von Berlin', a German offensive was prepared against the 61st Soviet Schützenkorps that lay between Frankfurt and Küstrin on the east bank of the river Oder. The ROA division was to play a limited role militarily, but a great psychological effect was expected. The main burden of the offensive would be borne by the 25th Pz.Gren.D. and the 'Führergrenadierdivision'.

The attack was finally launched on 27 March 1945. A handful of German divisions rushed towards Küstrin, but on 28 March, the OKW already concluded that the offensive had come to a standstill. The next day, the OKW diary reported that the Red Army had penetrated the centre of Küstrin. The ROA forces were not able to come into their own during these battles.

Melancholy in the battle of Erlenhof

On 8 April 1945 Vlassov was on a front-line visit to the troops. The situation was more than tense. The German plans to keep the Red Army east of the Oder proved unrealistic and Vlassov was afraid of fragmentation in the Russian liberation army. This put him in a difficult position with regard to the front commanders. The German commanders especially wanted to keep the 1st ROA-division, which was already deployed. Thus, Vlassov chose a middle way: the ROA division was available for short action with a limited goal and time frame, and would then join the Liberation Army.

Soviet troops proved themselves at the river Oder

ROA emblem

The Germans agreed, and the ROA forces were concentrated around the Soviet bridgehead 'Erlenhof'. This bridgehead, defended by well trained Soviet garrison troops, was an easy target. The bridgehead had already suffered from the German Fahnenjunkerregiment 1233 attacks, and the ROA troops were expected to deliver the final blow. General-major Bunjacenko of the Army of Liberation had observed the situation and called for extensive artillery and air support for the operation. He spoke of a 'hurricane-like preparation' and the deployment of some 28,000 shells. Given the lack of ammunition in those days, the chronicler of the Vlassov army, historian Joachim Hoffmann, characterised Bunjacenko's demand as 'exorbitant'. Another demand of the ROA leadership was that the Russians should carry out the attack alone, without German help. Thus, in the event of success, the credit would go entirely to the Vlassov forces.

The fact that the Germans agreed to all conditions, even the enormous artillery bombardment, showed how important this mission was to them. Major I.G. Schwenningen, looking back after the war, recalled that the ROA troops had been excellently equipped by Germany. The immediate preparation took place between Bunjacenko and the commander of the German Fahnenjunker regiment over a sumptuous Russian-style breakfast. They wanted to avoid a frontal attack across the wet open fields and a two-sided roll-up became the battle plan. The Fahnenjunkers would not participate in the attack on 'Erlenhof', but would distract the Soviet troops with mock offensive. The whole operation was given the operational name 'Unternehmen Aprilwetter'. The operation would start on 13 April 1945, with artillery support from several units, including SS-Artillerie-Regiment 32.

On the evening of 12^e the ROA fighters took up their positions. The slogan of the troops was "Gajl Vlassov" (Heil Vlassov). On 13 April, the artillery bombardment for 'Aprilwetter' started at 04.45 hours. The Soviet positions and the compounds on the Oder were surprised with a rain of fire. The German observer at the ROA, Oberstleutnant Von Notz, could not remember such a massive bombardment. The atmosphere was tense, since the future of the Vlassov initiative was at stake. The first signs were hopeful. Both on the north and south side, the ROA breakthrough succeeded. Soviet bunkers and positions were overrun. However, by noon, Soviet resistance grew. The Luftwaffe and ROA intervened with 26 aircraft.

Despite the support, the ROA troops were trapped in an endless web of barbed wire and under murderous artillery fire that threatened their flanks. ROA commander Bunjacenko, who at first had opposed the whole plan but finally agreed after German promises of help, now lost faith in operation 'Aprilwetter'. What probably played a role was the fact that Bunjacenko had foreseen a bloodbath, contrary to the 'short limited operation' promised by the Germans. The cunning Bunjacenko, according to the historian Joachim Hoffmann, managed to get his 20,000 men out of the operation more or less unscathed so that a reunion with the rest of the Vlassov army would be possible. The attack on the 'Erlenhof Bridgehead' was an illusion. The Vlassov initiative was again in a difficult phase.

Vlassov collects his troops near Prague

A miraculous development followed 'Aprilwetter'. Bunjacenko managed to move his infantry division hundreds of kilometres through devastated Europe to reunite with Vlassov's other units around Prague. The immediate German army command, General Theodor Busse, the commander of the German 9de army, played a miraculous role. He had called the ROA officers to account for their wayward actions at 'Aprilwetter', but Bunjacenko simply did not show up. This was downright refusal of command. It was unheard of and Busse was at a loss as to what to do, because the ROA division had simply left. The ROA getting away with it must have had something to do with the growing German disbelief in their own cause, but probably also with the prestige and politics surrounding Vlassov. People did not want to burn their hands on the new showpiece of the Reichsführer-SS. Ordinary military standards did not apply here. Busse only dared to go after the ROA politically. There were discussions with the OKH (Supreme Command of the Army) about disarming the 600th division, but in the end there was no resistance on the march south to Prague.

Bunjacenko's division made the long march south, past Dresden, Laun, towards Schlüsselburg (Lnare). During the retreat, the 600th division crossed several other

Bronislav Kaminski

German units. Sometimes they could have really used the ROA's help, but many German officers shied away from this and simply let the unit pass. It was a bizarre situation.

Following a final Karlsbad meeting, Vlassov himself feverishly continued to piece his unit together. New interesting initiatives were taken. Firstly, they tried to begin talks with the Western Allies via France. Secondly they tried to talk to Switzerland as a neutral power. And lastly, lines were also drawn to the Cetnik units, Yugoslav royalists under the command of General Draza Michajlovic, the plan being to retreat with them to the Yugoslav mountain areas and await the future. The ROA was both afraid of Stalin and worried about the Germans. There was also speculation about a breakthrough towards the underground Ukrainian freedom fighters of the UPA, but that seems unlikely due to the front situation.

Another option, which was becoming more and more topical, was to join forces with Czech resistance fighters. Vlassov had his reservations about this, as it meant betraying Germany just when the Germans were so lenient. In addition, he saw the Czech resistance as a messy and poorly organised 'fighting force', and figured that an amalgamation would be very risky from a military point of view. The best organised resistance in the Czech Republic had a communist orientation and they distrusted the Russian collaborators and vice versa.

In the course of April 1945, "National-Czech" resistance groups formed with which tougher agreements could be made. This was a right-wing initiative, suported by the police apparatus, around groups such as 'Kommando Alex', commanded by General Slunecko, the 'Greater Prague' group, and 'Bartos', led by General Kutvasr. Participation in the Prague national uprising could provide an unexpected way out for the Osttruppen.

Loyalty to Germany or hand in hand with the Czech resistance?

Internally, there were now fierce discussions within the Army of Liberation. Bunyacenko and his Chief of Staff Nikolaev were in favour of collaboration with the Czech Nationalists. Colonel Pozdnjakov had his reservations. All eyes turned to Vlassov. This also applied to the German side; his German staff officer, Erhard Kroeger, kept an eye on Vlassov. Kroeger believed Vlassov would keep his word, as he had remained faithful to his agreements so far. On the other hand, the building of an anti-fascist front in the Czech Republic did not conflict with Vlassov's ideals. The idea of keeping the front closed to the east was alluded to, so that the American troops could liberate Prague.

Everything indicated that Vlassov was in a strong internal conflict of conscience. He hoped for a German-Western Allied alliance against the Soviet Union, but this did not materialise. The internal consultations in the Russian liberation army became more and more emotional. There was pressure from many sides and Vlassov's authority was under threat. According to legend, Vlassov left the meeting with his fellow officers, saying: 'If my orders are no longer obeyed, I have no more business here.'

The practical consequence was that Vlassov tolerated Bunjacenko's movement towards the Czech resistance.

Kozak

This was also enforced by the course of events. On 5 May 1945, the Prague uprising had broken out. The Vlassov army had the choice of joining or becoming the enemy. A decision was made to do the former. Vlassov's betrayal of Germany was a fact. In no time, the German occupying forces in Prague were in trouble. On 8 May, the Germans were allowed to leave the city during a ceasefire.

Different versions circulate on the role of Vlassov troops in the outbreak of the Prague uprising. From a Communist point of view, Vlassov troops were only incidentally involved in the uprising. Chronologist Joachim Hoffmann characterised this as propaganda and saw a broader support for the Prague initiative. In their documentation, the Czech national forces also spoke openly of joining forces with the ROA soldiers against the Germans. In practice, it turned out that the 1st ROA division, the 600 I.D., had participated fully in the Prague uprising.

Bunjacenko was aware of the historic opportunity and did everything he could to make a good impression on the Czech national forces, for instance, executing an ROA soldier who had looted. Bunjacenko believed that in good ROA discipline lay "our honour and salvation". However, not everything went smoothly. A depot with fuel for the new German jets (Me-262) was captured by the ROA troops, and because they suspected that there was alcohol in the storage tanks, a drinking binge started which cost several ROA soldiers their lives. The Russian Liberation Army was a large army and discipline could not be maintained everywhere. Even before the May uprising in Prague, there had been a shoot-out between ROA troops and German soldiers at the Louny station after a dispute over fuel.

There was more courtesy between the German staff officers at Vlassov's headquarters and the Liberation Army: ROA soldiers apologised while disarming Major I.G. Schwenningen. Nikolaev even took the trouble to explain the Russian position to Schwenningen.

Battles between the Vlassov army and the Germans around Rosin

From a military point of view, the uprising in Prague was the most exciting on 6 May 1945. German units, which were still well organised and armed, were casuing the Czech freedom fighters trouble. Here, the ROA came to the rescue.

To avoid confusion with the Germans - after all, they were wearing the same uniform - the Russian tri-colour was attached to their arms. The fiercest fighting was done by the ROA around the German airfield Ruzyne (Rosin), from where the new Me-262-jet fighters were deployed. The German battle group 'Hogeback' defended the strategic base. The battle was preceded by several diplomatic attempts to resolve the matter non-violently. The chief of the VIII. Fliegenkorps' chief of staff, Oberst I.G. Sorge, went to the Russians himself for negotiations. 'My friend Vlassov will arrange this,' he thought naively. Unfortunately, the ROA took him prisoner and threatened to execute him if the airbase was not given up. The Germans did not give in and Sorge was executed.

For the Germans, this the tipping point. The last Me-262 jet-fighters were armed and used in a dive on the access roads where the columns of the Russian liberation army marched. As a counter-attack, the ROA

Vlassov gathered his Russians near Prague

troops took the airfield under fire, destroying the runways and thus its strategic importance.

Vlassov, meanwhile, was with the ROA's 2de division. Plans were developed to fly Vlassov to Franco's Spain to safety. However, Vlassov did not want to leave his men alone. In these final days he received a delegation of the Cossack units in Northern Italy. Vlassov ordered all units to march in the direction of Innsbruck. On 30 April 1945 there was another meeting between Kröger, as Köstering's envoy, and Vlassov, in Bad Reichenhall. Here, through the German general Schörner, another attempt was made to find a solution without bloodshed between the ROA and Berlin. Vlassov chose a practical solution. As long as the 2de division was not attacked, the ROA troops would not undertake any violence themselves.

Meanwhile, worrying reports came from Prague. The provisional government asked the Liberation Army why they had come to Prague. The ROA officers stated that it had been requested by the Czech resistance. 'The resistance is not the government,' was the answer. This made it clear that the Russians were in danger of falling between two stools. For Vlassov, it was clear that contact with the Americans had to be made as soon as possible.

At Przibram, south of Prague, there were new incidents with communist Czech resistance groups cooperating with the Red Army. A number of ROA soldiers were prisoners, but were forcibly freed by Vlassov troops. They were men who, under the ROA officer F. Truchin, had made contact with the approaching Americans. They had demanded that the liberating army surrender within 36 hours. However, on the way back from the

Roa-soldier

negotiations, the ROA officers were captured by Czech resistance and the Red Army. General J. Bojarksi was among the unfortunate ones who fell into the hands of the Red Army and he was hanged in Przibram.

It was clear that the Osttruppen had little to expect from the Red Army. General Truchin had disappeared without a trace. These were the chaotic final days of the Third Reich. On 30 April 1945, Hitler had committed suicide in the bunker in Berlin and on 7 May, the unconditional surrender of Nazi Germany was a fact. Because of this, all of Vlassov's plans fell apart.

The GIs in Pilsen

In Pilsen, Vlassov made contact with the Americans for the first time. The American major he reported to first thought he was dealing with an officer of the Red Army. The poor man had no idea of the existence of the Russian Liberation Army. This did not make Vlassov's negotiating position any easier. Another American officer was found, but he stated that it was beyond his authority to give guarantees about Vlassov and his men not being handed over to the Soviets. The only thing the ROA could do was to surrender without conditions.

The Americans treated their new Russian 'acquaintances' nonchalantly. Civilian clothing was available and Vlassov could have gotten away in it. However, he insisted that the fate of his troops be clear. At first, the Americans seemed to react rather 'humanly' to this strange group of Russians. They allowed him to rejoin the ROA troops who were now at Schlüsselburg. The Americans even supplied fuel for his car. In the streets Vlassov was recognised by Czech citizens. They saw him partly as the liberator of Prague and praise was everywhere. A woman threw a bouquet of flowers into the car.

In Schlüsselburg, the atmosphere changed. Vlassov was briefed and the American officer asked why he had fought against his fatherland. Vlassov was not interested in a lesson in history and stared stoically ahead. Vlassov was in any case a 'difficult man to read', which did not make contact easier. The Americans now tried to reassure him and replaced the word 'Russia' by the word 'Stalin'. They looked for motives. Finally the conversation took place, and a flaming speech by the Russian ROA-general. The Americans were impressed and seemed to want to help. The next day, 11 May, the ROA units were assembled 6 kilometres north of Schlüsselburg. Vlassov was given the opportunity by the Americans to escape to the English zone, but again Vlassov remained loyal to his troops. By evening, the Soviet armoured units were already in front of Vlassov's unit.

Shortly afterwards, the first contacts were made. The Soviet commander promised the ROA troops security. But Vlassov and his men knew better. It had become clear that the Americans would not accept the Army of Liberation. They had their backs against the wall. Sven Steenberg sketched the situation: the Vlassov army, until then orderly, literally fell apart in minutes. Everyone wanted to leave, the wild flight had begun. Nobody wanted to fall into the hands of the Soviets. The great hunt for the Vlassov troops had begun. Soviets and communist Czechs participated fully. It was the beginning of a bloodbath. Executions took place at random. Possibly 10,000 ROA soldiers lost their lives in the May chaos.

Vlassov wrote one last memorandum, saying he was prepared to answer before an independent tribunal. But led by an American armoured car, a convoy with the top of the ROA headed east, towards the Russians. As soon as the Soviets had sight of Vlassov, machine guns were pointed at him. Vlassov spread his arms and said calmly, 'You can shoot.' The Americans just stood there, petrified.

Swallowed up by Yalta

In Yalta, agreements were made between the Allies: the Soviet collaborators had to be extradited on that basis. The two ROA divisions suffered this fate. The staff of the 2de division surrendered only after a firefight. The commander's wife took the poison pill. The Cossack corps that had tried to unite itself with the Vlassov units was located on the Drau River near the Austrian border. They thus fell under British rule and were gathered around Weitensfeld. Here, the threat of extradition made the Cossacks go on a hunger strike. However, this could not prevent the extradition from taking place. This lasted until the beginning of June 1945, when 37 gener-

The Soviet regime ruthlessly dealt with collaborators

General Helmuth von Pannwitz

Caucasian volunteers

als, 2,200 officers and more than 30,000 cossacks were extradited. There were dramatic scenes of suicide and desperate people throwing themselves into the Drau. Meanwhile, the local population plundered the camp left behind, horses were captured and everything of value disappeared. The British officer Major Davis, who led the extradition to the Soviets, announced through a megaphone that he admired the Cossacks' fight for freedom, but was forced to extradite them due to international agreements.

On 12 August 1946 and on 17 January 1947, the trials of Soviet collaborators were completed by the Soviets. They were almost laconic announcements. The leadership of the ROA and the Cossack units were simply sentenced to the noose. When the message reached the newspapers, the sentences had already been carried out. Vlassov was condemned and erased from history, along with supporters such as Malischkin, Schilenkov, Truchin and others.

ROA soldier

The 162ste Turk-Division was also handed over by the British to the Soviets and suffered the same fate. General Pannwitz fell into Russian hands and, after his capitulation on 11 May, was handed over to the Red Army and executed in January 1947. In 1997, he was rehabilitated by Yeltsin as a 'victim of Stalinism'. Oberländer was one of the few who managed to break through to the West. He would become a minister under Chancellor Adenauer.

Afterword: difficult balance sheet

It is difficult to painted an accurate picture of the Osttruppen. It is still a painful subject in the debate surrounding the history of the war in Eastern Europe. Von Pannwitz, as we saw, was rehabilitated under Russian President Boris Yeltsin, and today there are hundreds of statues of Bandera in the Ukraine. The collaborators were praised for their anti-communism, but there was also the dark side. They had collaborated and they had blood on their hands. They were partly equated with the Nazis and persecuted, or even liquidated a few years after the war, which happened to Stefan Bandera when he was liquidated by the Soviet secret service in Munich in 1959.

All the sensitive contradictions were already at play during the war itself. The Germans appealed to the ideal of freedom of the collaborating nations, but at the same time suppressed them because of Germany's own strategy. In addition to being brothers in arms, the allies were also seen as 'Untermenschen'. This was a permanent and painful paradox, despite the fact that some German commanders identified themselves with the Osttruppen and did everything in their power to support them in their wishes and endeavours, as was the case with Von Pannwitz, Oberländer and Von Heygendorff, the last commander of the 162ste Turk-Division. As a result of all this, Gerhard von Mende estimated that some one million Russian men served in the German army or auxiliary battalions. At times, 10% of the army on the Eastern Front consisted of 'Russians'. These Russians were in fact representatives of many peoples. Von Mende believed that 180,000 Turkmen had served under the Germans, 110,000 Caucasian, 40,000 Tatar and hundreds of thousands of others, including Russians and Ukrainians. These men had made a great blood sacrifice for their collaboration. Von Mende calculated that the Caucasians alone left about 48% of their volunteers some 50,000 dead on the battlefield.

The discussion about the collaboration of the Osttruppen was revived during the battle over the Donuch coal mine between Vladimir Putin and present-day Ukraine. In the war propaganda, demons from the past were brought back to life.

The Ukrainian troops were portrayed as 'fascists' by Moscow. Some Ukrainian loners saw this as a badge of honour and decorated themselves with fascist symbolism.

The lack of democratic tradition in the region is eating through it. That is why the last word will not yet be written on this issue, which will continue to watch over the history of the Second World War in Eastern Europe.

Concise literature review:

Alvarez, M.G./Pierik, P., *De Spaanse blauwe divisie. De dramatische strijd van Franco's troepen voor Leningrad*, Soesterberg: uitgeverij Aspekt 2021 (tweede druk)

Baumeister, R., *Erfahrungen mit Ostfreiwilligen im II. Weltkrieg, In: Wehrkunde, Organ der Gesellschaft für Wehrkunde*, IV.jahrgang 1955

Beld, A., *Met Hitler tegen Stalin. Samenwerking met de Duitse bezetter in de Sovjet-Unie,* Soesterberg; Uitgeverij Aspekt, 2021

Bethell, N., *The Last Secret. The Delivery too Stalin of over two million Russians by Britain and the United States*, New York: Basic Books

Cwiklinski, S., Die Panturkismus der SS: Angehörige sowjetischer Turkvöker als Objekte und Subjekte der SS Politik In: Zentrum Moderner Orient, geisteswissenschaftliche Zentern Berlin e.V., Gerhard Höp und Brigitte Reinwald (hg.), *Fremdeinsätze, Afrikaner und Asiaten in europaischen Kriegen, 1914-1918 Studien 13 Berlin:* Verlag das Arabische Buch, 2000

Dallin, A., *Deutsche Herrschaft in Russland*, Düsseldorf: Droste Verlag 1958

Dossena, P.A., Hitler's *Turkestani Soldiers. A History of the 162nd (Turkistan) Infantry Division* Solihull: Helion & Company 2015

Fleischhauer, E.I., *Der Kapp-Putsch. Lenin und Ludendorff 1918-1920*, Edition Winterwork, 2020

Heike, W.D., *Sie wollten die Freiheit. Die Geschichte der Ukrainischen Division 1943-1945* Dorheim: Podzun verlag z.j.

Hoffmann, J., *Die Tragödie der Russische Befreiungsarmee 1944/45. Wlassow gegen Stalin* Herbig Verlag 1984

Hoffmann, J., *Deutsche und Kalmyken 1942-bis 1945*, Freiburg: Rombach Verlag

Lower, W., *Nazi Empire-Building and the Holocaust in Ukraine*, The University of North Carolina Press 2005

Mackiewicz, J., *Die Tragödie an der Drau. Die verratene Freiheit*, München: Bergstadtverlag 1957

Mende, G. Von, Errfahrungen mit Ostfreiwilligen in der deutschen Wehrmacht während des Zweiten Weltkrieges, In: *Auslandforschung, Schriftenreihe der Auslandwissenschaftlichen Gesellschaft e.V. Heft 1, Vielvöker-Heere und Koalitions-Kriege*. Darmstad: C.W.Leske Verlag 1952

Michaelis, R., *Ukrainer in der Waffen-SS. Die 14. Waffen-Grenadier-Division der SS (ukrainische nr. 1)*, Berlin: Michaelis-Verlag 2000

Nahaylo, B., Ukrainian National Resistance in Soviet Ukraine during the 1920s, In: *Journal of Ukrainian Studies 15, No 2 Winter 1990*

Pierik, P., *'Neu Turkestan' aan het front. Islamitische soldaten uit de Kaukasus en de Balkan in dienst van de Waffen-SS*, Soesterberg: uitgeverij Aspekt 2019

Pierik, P., *Het Rode Leger wankelt. Ruslandveldtocht 1941*, Soesterberg: uitgeverij Aspekt 2015

Pierik, P., *Krim. Bestorming, belegering, verovering, bezetting en moord. 1941-1942*, Soesterberg: uitgeverij Aspekt 2021 (tweede druk)

Pierik, P., *Horthy en de strijd om de Hongaarse natiestaat. Over de oorsprong van het anti-Europa sentiment in Hongarije*, Soesterberg: uitgeverij Aspekt, 2021

Pierik, P., *Wapenbroeders. Roemenië nazi-Duitsland en operatie 'Barbarossa'*, Soesterberg: uitgeverij Aspekt 2021

Rudling, P.A., The Defended Ukraine: The 14.Waffen-Grenadier-Division der SS (Galizische Nr.1) revisited, In: *The Journal of Slavic Military Studies 04.09.2012*

Schnell, F., *Räume des Schreckens. Gewalt und Gruppenmilitanz in der Ukraine 1905-1933*, Hamburg: Hamburger edition 2012

Steenberg, S., *Verräter oder Patriot? Wlassow.* Köln: Verlag Wissenschaft und Polik, 1968

Sudoplatov, P. Sudoplatov, A., *Special Task. The Memoirs of an unwanted witness- a Soviet Spymaster,* Boston/New York: 1994

Vynnychenko, I., The Deportation, Incarceration and forced Resettlement of Ukrainians in the Soviet Period, In: *Journal of Ukrainian Studies 18 no 1-2 (Summer-Winter 1993)*

Archives:

Germandocsinrussia: Bestandbuch 500 Findbuch 12463, Akte 48 Bestandbuch 500 Findbuch 12454 Akte 376, Bestandbuch 500 Findbuch 12469, Akte 5, Bestandbuch 500 Findbuch 12470, Akte 2, Bestandbuch 500, Findbuch 12646, Akte 169, Bestandbuch 500 Findbuch 12477 Akte 25 Bestandbuch 500, Findbuch 12451 Akte 24, Bestandbuch 500, Findbuch 12451 Akte 376

National Archives Washington: T78/R413, T78/R541, T84/R245, T313/R172, T175/R104, T311/R236, T314/R31, T314/R831, T314/R1050, T315/R412, T501/R203, T501/R350